At David C Cook, we equip the local church around the corner and around the globe to make disciples. Come see how we are working together—go to **www.davidccook.com**. Thank you!

transforming lives together

What people are saying about …

THE FRESH EYES SERIES

"I heard Doug speak over a decade ago on the feeding of the five thousand, and I still remember what he said. He brought the familiar story to life in a way that made me see it all unfold. I remember thinking, *What would I have done if I'd been there that day with Jesus?* That's why Doug's writing is so valuable. God recorded these events in His Word and Doug takes readers to those moments in history and makes them relatable and best of all, memorable."

—**Robin Jones Gunn**, bestselling author
of over ninety books including the Christy
Miller series and *Victim of Grace*

"On a visit to Japan, our translator asked an artist working in gold leaf how it felt to be surrounded by such expensive materials. The artist replied, 'I've been working with gold so long, I've forgotten it's value.' I know I've felt that exact way when it comes to reading the Word of God. I've been working/reading/studying it for so long, I'm ashamed to say that sometimes, even though I love God's Word, I've forgotten it's value. That's why I'm so grateful for Fresh Eyes. Doug has taken the familiar stories of Scripture, and given us new ideas to ponder, angles to look from, and context to understand. A reminder of the richness and value that surrounds us every day."

—**Kathi Lipp**, bestselling author of *The Husband Project*, *Clutter Free*, and *Overwhelmed*

"The Fresh Eyes series is nothing less than amazing—the most profound, to the point, original, awe-inspiring, and challenging writings about Jesus and the Bible I have ever read or imagined! I was immediately stunned by how the subject matter is exactly what I've always been looking for in Scripture! I hope there will be millions of Christians like me who learn to see Scripture with fresh eyes."

—**Jorge Casas**, bassist, Grammy-award winning producer

"These books are a hit. Doug has found a profound and compelling way to have the reader (ordinary people like you and me) have the eyes of our hearts enlightened. I have read the entire Bible, front to back, for the past fourteen years. In these books, I have gained new insight into Bible sayings, Jesus' miracles, and Jesus' parables. I gained fresh insight into what God is saying to me. In my 162 MLB game schedule, each day brings new excitement. Doug's writing and dissecting of verses make each verse exciting as I grew deeper in my relationship with our Lord."

—**David Jauss**, Major League baseball coach, Pittsburgh Pirates

"Jesus spoke of unique teachers who were able to bring 'new treasures' out of their storerooms (Matt. 13:52). Doug Newton is an extraordinary author who brings us 'new treasure' in this Fresh Eyes series. This series imparts the rare gift of seeing Scripture with fresh eyes, thus igniting fresh fire in our lives for Jesus and His mission. I highly recommend this series for anyone desiring a personal revival and an expanded faith for how greatly God can use their lives. I experienced this for myself as I read Doug's life-giving words!"

—**Larry Walkemeyer**, D.Min.; pastor; church planter; Director of Equipping—Exponential; author of *15 Characteristics of Effective Pastors*

"Doug Newton is a skilled and passionate communicator as well as a trusted, wise guide both from the pulpit and the printed page. His Fresh Eyes series draws from clear thought, engaged storytelling, and a worthy message to help readers marvel anew over God's love and sustain their faith in the face of today's challenges."

—**Ivan L. Filby**, PhD, president of Greenville University, IL

"For many who cherish the Bible as God's Word, a daily experience with the Bible has no greater impact than a weather report, an Op-Ed piece, or a blog post. This is because few believers actually read the Bible much and, when they do, they give it only superficial attention. In the Fresh Eyes series, Doug Newton demonstrates how familiar miracle stories, well-known parables, and often-cited gospel sayings can come alive with power to expose small and limited horizons and expand them to wider and deeper perceptions of kingdom reality then draw you in as Newton teases out life-changing biblical implications."

—**Bishop David W. Kendall**, PhD, Free Methodist Church—USA

"For decades Doug Newton's clear and crisp teaching has captured the deep and transformative truths of God's Word. What a treasure to have these rich and wonderful insights through Fresh Eyes. You will be deeply touched and truly challenged by this brilliant master teacher. What a gift!"

—**David Goodnight**, JD, LLM,
partner at Stoel Rives, LLP

"Doug Newton reminds us that the compelling teachings and miracles of Jesus were not just clever events to create believers but were the examples of everyday life. In captivating stories, Newton refocuses us to remember that staying tuned in in prayerful communion opens our eyes to the reality that miracles happen all around us all the time."

—**Hal Conklin**, president of USA
Green Communities, former mayor
of Santa Barbara, California

"Fresh Eyes is a crucial series for our hyper-connected world. Doug Newton equips readers with the tools needed to slow down, open our eyes, and unlock the true meaning of the inspired stories of the Bible. As he has done from the pulpit for many years, Doug provides rich guidance and training with easy-to-understand language and stories that make things click. Fresh Eyes is a must-have for anyone who wants to be equipped to wrestle with the meaning of Scripture and the many ways it applies to the hustle and bustle of twenty-first-century living.

—**Hugo Perez**, chief marketing
officer, OHorizons Foundation

F R E S H

E Y E S

O N

JESUS'
PARABLES

Discovering New Insights in Familiar Passages

DAVID **C** COOK

transforming lives together

FRESH EYES ON JESUS' PARABLES
Published by David C Cook
4050 Lee Vance Drive
Colorado Springs, CO 80918 U.S.A.

Integrity Music Limited, a Division of David C Cook
Eastbourne, East Sussex BN23 6NT, England

The graphic circle C logo is a registered trademark of David C Cook.

Unless otherwise noted, all Scripture quotations are taken from THE HOLY
BIBLE, NEW INTERNATIONAL VERSION, NIV Copyright © 1973,
1978, 1984, 2011 by Biblica, Inc. Used by permission. All rights reserved
worldwide. Scripture quotations marked ESV are taken from the ESV Bible
(The Holy Bible, English Standard Version), copyright © 2001 by Crossway,
a publishing ministry of Good News Publishers. Used by permission. All
rights reserved; NKJV are taken from the New King James Version. Copyright
© 1982 by Thomas Nelson. Used by permission. All rights reserved.
The author has added italics to Scripture quotations for emphasis.

LCCN 2018931980
ISBN 978-1-4347-1212-7
eISBN 978-1-4347-1215-8

© 2018 Douglas M. Newton
Published in association with the literary agency of Books & Such
Literary Management, 52 Mission Circle, Suite 122, PMB 170,
Santa Rosa, CA 95409-5370, www.booksandsuch.com.

The Team: Alice Crider, Mick Silva, Amy Konyndyk,
Rachael Stevenson, Diane Gardner, Susan Murdock
Cover Design: Nick Lee

Printed in the United States of America
First Edition 2018

1 2 3 4 5 6 7 8 9 10

051618

To the late Dr. Larry Mayhew, philosopher,
who ignited my passion for clear thinking
and writing when I turned in a two-page,
double-spaced reflection paper on Descartes's
"cogito, ergo sum" and he returned a three-page,
single-spaced critique of every sentence I wrote!

CONTENTS

ACKNOWLEDGMENTS

The man who was, I think, the most creative and engaging preacher I ever heard died in a car crash when I was in sixth grade. I say "I think" because I never really cared about what he was saying at the time. After all, I was only twelve years old, and there were better things to do to pass the time until noon. But I sensed his impact because of the way my parents and all the other adults in my small country church reacted when he preached. They loved it—and him. The congregation leaned forward. Even our 1965 Chevy Impala seemed eager for church every Sunday!

Carl Johnson, our pastor, a journalism grad student at Syracuse University, apparently mixed humor with ways to enter a biblical text that disposed of the traditional three-point sermon with the tearjerker story at the end. Again I say "apparently" because I didn't get the jokes or insights; I just heard the appreciative laughs and appreciable amens around me.

And even though I vowed at age ten I would never be a preacher, I knew what a preacher needed to be from sitting in the pews Sunday after Sunday inside that atmosphere of rapt attention. So when I did eventually become a pastor-teacher—even though my "call" was initially more coincidental than covenantal—I had an unchosen but unwavering passion: to help people see the Bible with fresh eyes and expectancy.

Now that forty years of preaching and teaching have passed, I can see how the "spirit" of Carl Johnson—I should really capitalize that word—permeated and still permeates how I approach biblical examination and exposition. That Spirit led me to preach two back-to-back sermons one Sunday while running the entire time on a treadmill in order to illustrate the significance of Peter's use of the word *spoudazo* (meaning "make every effort") in 2 Peter 1:5. It led me to build and preach inside a black cloth-covered enclosure just so I could come to the finale and demonstrate with one thrust of a spear how praise and proclamation pierce spiritual darkness.

I never wanted to use gimmicks, but very often the Lord prompted me to see something unusual and use something visual. As a result, I have enjoyed kind comments from the people of four congregations over the years telling me how much they looked forward to what I was going to do and say on Sunday. I always deflected those comments with "You mean, what the *Lord* is going to say." And they would nod, "Of course."

However, the fact remains that the human role of careful study and creativity combine to make what God wants to say through His Word clear and compelling. Creativity is inherently mnemonic.

At the outset of this Fresh Eyes series, I want to acknowledge Carl Johnson and the gifted thinkers and teachers he represents who have inspired me toward preaching that reveals rather than regurgitates truth. And even more, I thank all the congregations of believers among whom I have lived and served who have shown me what it looks like to lean forward to hear a word from the Lord: for three years with the kids of the South Presbyterian Church high school group in Syracuse, New York; for thirteen years with the people of Fountain Square Church in Bowling Green, Kentucky; for five years with the students and staff of the Oakdale Christian Academy boarding school in Jackson, Kentucky; and for the past eleven years with the people of Greenville (IL) Free Methodist Church.

For fifteen years I served as editor of *Light & Life*, the denominational magazine of the Free Methodist Church. This was also a significant time in my life when I learned to communicate more broadly through writing to people I would never see from the Sunday pulpit. That opportunity and training would never have occurred without the courage of four bishops who hired me—a pastor with no journalism or seminary degree—simply because I had what they regarded as an anointed, albeit "unsafe" (their word), creative approach to communication.

My role as editor led to my speaking periodically at writer's conferences—most often at the renowned Mount Hermon Christian Writers Conference. I owe a great debt of thanks to Dave Talbott, who hardly knew me when inviting me to preach on Palm Sunday in 1998 in the rustic auditorium beneath the praising redwoods to the crowd filled with professional writers. And he continued to do so for several years, even though I had not yet joined the ranks of published authors.

That is where I was first heard and shaped by these professionals, many of whom became friends. One of them, Wendy Lawton, committed herself to me as my agent long before there was any sign I would ever repay her kindness with even a dime of compensation. I couldn't have been given a more gifted, wise, and dedicated agent than she and the Books & Such Literary Agency.

One day she and Janet Grant, founder of the agency, approached me with a clear vision of how to position me as an author. They said, "You need to just do what you do—open people's eyes to Scripture in fresh ways." Within a few months, I had a contract with David C Cook thanks to them and Alice Crider, senior acquisitions editor, who championed this multi-book project with an accompanying app.

Suddenly I had a contract, and the initial draft of three books had to be written from scratch in five months. This was a daunting task made more feasible, because over the years I have learned how to write with intense focus as my Greenville church staff graciously accommodated my need to get away several times a year to work on various writing projects.

However, when this massive project came along I needed something more than intense focus. I would need big blocks of time and a sense of the Lord's permission. A series of God-ordained events gave me that green light and changed my ministry responsibilities dramatically. Two of those events involved divine instruction that came miraculously and separately through Ben Dodson and Sarah Vanderkwaak. I am grateful they risked speaking when they could have remained silent. I am also grateful for dear friends Ivan and Kathie Filby, and my gifted superintendent Ben Tolly, for seeing a future ahead of me I would not have imagined.

Alice Crider was gracious enough to honor my request to select my own editor, Mick Silva. We had met at Mount Hermon and had only two casual conversations, but that was enough for me to have confidence in his spiritual sensitivity and professional skills. This initial confidence proved to be well-founded as our friendship grew and as Mick's expertise sharpened and supported the mission and message of the Fresh Eyes books chapter by chapter and line by line.

I was also pleased to have been brought into the David C Cook family at a time when the company was retooling its focus and functions in fresh ways to fulfill its longstanding mission to resource and disciple the church worldwide. That mission, so evident in the processes and people at David C Cook, convinced my wife and me to come under their banner in this project. I have enjoyed how much I have learned every step of the way through the enthusiastic encouragement of Alice Crider, Toben Heim, and the team of people assigned to guide me through this project to completion and distribution: Rachael Stevenson, Diane Gardner,

Kayla Fenstermaker, Amy Konyndyk, Nick Lee, Susan Murdock, Megan Stengel, Annette Brickbealer, Nathan Landry, and Austin Davco.

Finally, it probably goes without saying, but it is impossible not to shout from the rooftops how much I owe to my family. My two girls, their amazing husbands, and combined five kids. They have not only given me their love and respect over the years, but also what it means to live life knowing your kids are proud of you—and tell you! That lubricates the mechanics of life through the grind of large projects like Fresh Eyes.

Then there's Margie. She's my hero, my model, my friend, my encourager. There has been a sparkle in her eyes from the very beginning of being "us" that comes from her love for Jesus. That sparkle is my north star. It keeps me navigating through life, no matter what comes, toward greater love for the Lord. Without that sparkle in her eyes, my own would have long since grown dim with cares and worries and doubts preventing me from seeing anything—life itself and its Author—with fresh eyes. But when you have someone who loves you unconditionally in such a way that helps you know the love of God, your eyes will sparkle too with expectancy for seeing new and fresh things in the world and in the Word.

Doug Newton

March 2018

ABOUT THE FRESH
EYES SERIES

What if the commonplace understanding of a Bible story or a well-known Scripture passage is the very thing keeping us from seeing the text in a new, life-transforming way?

We all find ourselves facing this problem when we study the Bible. We believe Scripture is living and powerful. But many of us, after a genuine encounter with God followed by faithful Bible study and many sermons, became so familiar with Scripture that it lost its impact. The Bible became a book of riddles to be solved. Once we "figured out what a passage meant," we checked it off and moved on. We've seen these stories too many times, and everyone who's been a Christian for even a year or two knows how that voracious appetite for the Word quickly fades.

Pastors and Bible teachers craft a message from a particular text, and the lesson they convey becomes the way we understand the passage from that point on. Within a few short years, it feels like we're hearing the same thing over and over again. We begin to approach the Bible with less zip and zeal. Familiarity may not always breed contempt, but it does tend to breed complacency.

Yet consider Jesus' remedy: "You have heard that it was said, but I tell you …" He invited His listeners to break away from well-worn thinking to see something new, different. We need to look with fresh eyes at what we think we know well. A passage's common interpretation may have taken a wrong turn somewhere along the line and been passed along like an urban legend. The application may need to shift in a different direction or include something not considered before. There's new hope for our lives to change when we can say, "I never saw it that way before."

My primary mission with this book series is not to share new insights I've uncovered. My greater desire is to reveal specific techniques that will allow you to make new discoveries about familiar passages that can revive your love for the infinite Word and transform your work in teaching and testimony.

The interactive section at the end of each chapter includes a "Vision Check," which describes Fresh Eyes study techniques. These reveal how I found something new and inspiring by reexamining the text and context of a passage, the life situations involved, the cultural perspectives reflected, and other details and how I began to see Scripture more imaginatively. You'll also find more resources at dougnewton.com and on the Fresh Eyes app to help you gain additional insights.

I pray you find that the treasures in God's Word are truly inexhaustible when you come with fresh eyes.

INTRODUCTION

One Easter Sunday, I wanted to help my congregation powerfully sense the resurrection's importance and truly *feel* the impact of Paul's words in 1 Corinthians 15:17, 19: "If Christ has not been raised, your faith is futile; you are still in your sins…. We are of all people most to be pitied." I could have let them try to understand the significance of those words intellectually, but I wanted them to feel it in their guts and see that text with fresh eyes. So I decided to go the extra mile and do something I rarely did: I built a big prop to bring on stage—a wooden wall with a real glass window in it.

I placed the reinforced partition on the platform behind me to create my perfect visual aid, certain it would be a memorable picture of why the resurrection matters so much and why we have to reconsider the Bible's familiar-sounding words. I planned to take objects representing portions of the service—a hymnal for after singing the first hymn, a Bible for after the responsive reading, even offering plates—and chuck them out the window. It was going to be great.

So after we sang the first triumphant hymn, I held up the hymnal and said, "If Christ has not been raised from the dead, then we might as well take this hymnal"—I held it higher—"and *chuck it out the window!*" I drew back and let it fly. A loud crash resounded as the heavy songbook broke through the plate glass, producing a great dramatic effect.

The audible gasps followed by scattered laughter told me I'd gotten my wish.

The Word of God is immeasurably precious. We should never get so comfortable with any passage that we cease to see its ongoing creative possibilities. We can ask the Lord to give us fresh eyes to see something about a text—its meaning, context, credibility, power, or applicability—that we've never seen before. This is especially important when it comes to Jesus' parables.

Pioneering scholar C. H. Dodd said a "parable is a metaphor or simile" that "[arrests] the hearer by its vividness or strangeness … leaving the mind in sufficient doubt about its precise application to tease it into active thought."[1] Jesus wanted His followers—then and now—to grapple with these wonderful stories.

I want to help you do that through this book. Since parables are stories that use symbols and analogies, each text's meaning cannot always be pinned down like a butterfly in a collector's showcase. Instead, parables must be observed and allowed to float on the invisible currents of the imagination. While it is always worthwhile to ask, "What did Jesus mean?" Jesus' characteristic reluctance to provide the meaning suggests that a more important question may be, "What does it make you think about?"

Throughout church history, the parables' open-ended quality often resulted in disagreement. For several hundred years, early Christian leaders treated them like allegories in which each element represents something else. They pointed to Jesus' interpretation of the parable of the sower as a prime example of how to relate to parables (Matt. 13:1–23).

Admittedly, some bizarre interpretations came out of this and skewed the stories' purpose and intent. Bishop Irenaeus, for example, claimed the parable of the workers in Matthew 20 represents people saved at different times in history and the denarius represents eternal life.[2] Other scholars have argued that a parable should be reduced to one simple lesson. Seminary students are often trained in that school of thought. Thankfully, a resurgence of interpretation theories has allowed for allegorical readings of parables and their ability to convey multiple points at once.

Discussions of form, redaction, or literary criticism aim for the pearl of great price—the indisputably perfect approach to interpretation—but that's not what you'll find here. There's no conclusive agreement about how to interpret parables, and I start by assuming that this is actually a good thing, fitting for parables intended for ordinary folks like you and me. We need to use our limited permission and let the parables take us into Spirit-guided research, reflection, and application, in harmony with the whole Word of God.

We need to look at familiar parables in fresh ways. In a couple cases, we'll consider alternatives to the conventional interpretation. In others, a careful reading of the surrounding context may make the parable more compelling or convicting. Sometimes, the fuller lessons have increased my wonder over the gospel's promise or generated deeper implications. The last chapter in particular demonstrates how these narratives can expand to include reasonable hypothetical situations and reveal insights not noticed before.

The elasticity of the parables excites me. Even more, though some parables are suspected to be inauthentic, they have deepened my love for—and even my "Trinitarian" view of—God's Word. I'm very confident in Scripture's ability and credibility to show itself the bona fide Word of God to you in this book.

The apostle Paul regularly prayed for people to be given the Spirit of wisdom and revelation through having the eyes of their hearts enlightened (Eph. 1:17–18). Ultimately, that's what it takes to have "fresh eyes." But we need to do our part. If you're ready to discover your part, I invite you to read the parables of Jesus with fresh eyes.

1

"HELLO, TURKEY"

The Hidden Treasure
Matthew 13:44

How can one little Bible verse capture
the full meaning of salvation?

I grew up well before the era of iPads. The closest thing we had to an attention-grabbing flat-screen instrument was an Etch A Sketch. Remember? You drew on it by turning two knobs that moved an interior stylus against the backside of a gray screen, leaving a black line. If you got good at it, you could draw almost anything, and then you simply erased the screen and started over by turning it upside down and shaking it vigorously.

This is similar to what we often must do with our minds in order to see something new or even better in a familiar Scripture passage. Case in point: "The kingdom of heaven is like treasure hidden in a field. When a man found it, he hid it again, and then in his joy went and sold all he had and bought that field" (Matt. 13:44).

One common interpretation has been "Etch A Sketched" into our minds by preachers dialing in this point: the kingdom of heaven is such a precious treasure that we, like the man, should give up everything to lay hold of it. Of course, that's absolutely true—but probably not what Jesus was talking about. So let's flip our minds upside down, shake out the old teaching, and ask the Holy Spirit to help us discover something new. Let's start with a quick review of the facts:

- *What did the man buy?* Don't say "treasure." He wanted the treasure, but he had to buy the field where he found it in order to possess the treasure. That's an important observation.

- *How did the man come up with the money to buy the field?* He sold everything he owned.

- *What was his frame of mind while doing that?* He was joyful.

- *Finally, what was the kingdom of heaven like?* Wait … don't say "treasure." The first thing you must do whenever you approach a parable that begins "the kingdom of heaven (or God) is like …" is to put the parable's elements inside a parenthesis so the phrase "kingdom of heaven" applies to everything that follows. This parable is not saying the kingdom of God is like any *one* element in the parable, such as the treasure or the man or the field. Rather, the parable is saying the whole picture that follows is what the kingdom of God is like. That is, the man finds treasure, hides it, joyfully sells everything, and buys the field. Given that basic rule of interpretation, we cannot interpret this parable the common way—that the kingdom of God should be like a treasure to us.

You might then be tempted to ask, "So what is this parable telling us to value so highly that we would give up everything to obtain it?" Here's the bad news. If you ask the question that way, you'll never arrive at the answer, because too often we don't notice any unwarranted assumptions we make. Let me demonstrate by telling you a story.

For more than thirty years, I have asked groups to solve the following "twenty-questions mystery": Mary lies dead on the floor. Tom is asleep on the couch. A colorless, odorless liquid surrounds Mary's body, and broken pieces of glass are also scattered around her. The windows and doors are all locked from the inside. What happened?

The groups always start out with the same kinds of questions. Someone asks, "Has Mary been dead a long time?"

"No, but that's not relevant to the solution," I reply.

Another person asks, "The windows may be locked, but are any of them broken?"

"Clever question. But no, none of them are broken."

"Is the liquid water?"

"Yes."

"Did Mary drop the glass before she died, because she got frightened?"

"No," I say. "But you're making an unwarranted assumption."

Eyes squint and brows furrow. Questions fly: "Is it really a house?" "Is Tom really asleep?"

"Yes," I say, "but go beyond the facts you were presented with. Who are you assuming Mary is?"

A nurse? A murderer? A thief? Eventually someone hits on it: "Is Mary a woman?"

"No." I see the light turn on.

"A little girl?"

"No."

"Is Mary human?"

"No." And there it is.

From this point, the solution comes quickly: Tom is a cat. Mary is a goldfish. Tom knocked the fishbowl off the table, it broke, and Mary died.

In the same way, our unwarranted assumption about "the man" in this parable keeps us from understanding what Jesus was teaching about God's kingdom. Here's your hint: Who are you assuming the main character to be? What if the man who bought the field is not an ordinary human being like us but the Son of God?

CHRISTUS VICTOR

What if this isn't a parable about all we must do to possess the kingdom? What if Jesus is the one who finds the treasure? What if we human beings are the treasure? What if the field is this world that belonged to Satan, the former prince of the world? And what if it is Jesus who gives up everything He owns to purchase (redeem) this world and reclaim us as His possession? What if that's what the kingdom of heaven is like?

Did you realize that for the first thousand years of Christendom that picture was likely the more common way of understanding salvation? It is sometimes called *Christus Victor*. Today the common view is *penal substitution*: that is, Jesus died in our place to pay for our sins. This view of salvation has its roots in a classic atonement theory Saint Anselm articulated in the eleventh century. After various revisions following the Protestant Reformation, it has become the dominant view of salvation. It's not that Christus Victor is right and penal substitution is wrong. They simply represent different ways of looking at the gospel. God's work of salvation is so great (Heb. 2:3), like a huge mountain, that we must view it from many angles to gain an accurate and comprehensive picture. But most Christians don't realize this and believe there is only one way to describe what Jesus accomplished on the cross.

You could summarize the Christus Victor view of salvation this way: the prince of the world, Satan, possessed this world; the Son of God came to earth and defeated him on the cross, then established and commissioned the church to enforce His kingdom's rule on earth and reclaim lost people to His possession. That used to be a more common way to understand the gospel of salvation.

When I first viewed this parable from that angle, my whole idea of salvation expanded. However, I sensed the change was so big, it was important to check my new insight against Scripture. When I did, this short parable seemed to condense several verses about Jesus' death found in Hebrews and Paul's letters:

1. ... *then in his joy went*—"For the joy set before him he endured the cross ..." (Heb. 12:2).

2. ... *and sold all he had*—"[He] did not consider equality with God something to be used to his own advantage; rather, he made himself nothing ..." (Phil. 2:6–7).

3. ... *and bought that field*—"You are not your own; you were bought at a price" (1 Cor. 6:19–20).

So my new insight checked out. As a result, I now believe penal substitution is one way to understand the gospel, but

Christus Victor is also, and it may be the most glorious understanding we have. The King of the universe reclaimed this fallen
world. Isn't that exactly what Handel wrote in his celebrated
"Hallelujah Chorus"?

> The kingdom of this world
> Is become the kingdom of our Lord
> And of His Christ, and of His Christ;
> and He shall reign for ever and ever.[1]

Plus, rethinking my assumptions about this parable not
only resized my view of salvation but also upsized my longing
to join the Lord in His treasure-seeking work. For this parable
reveals our Lord's passion to reclaim us—you and me—as treasures that belong to Him. It tells of the lengths to which He will
go to make a person—any person—His.

HOW FAR JESUS GOES

A couple years ago after church, a somewhat-unkempt and
heavily tattooed young mom came up to me and my wife after
having waited for people to clear out. Unfamiliar with church
lingo and protocol, she asked cautiously, "You know your talk
today?" (She didn't call it a sermon.) "Why did you look toward
me and say 'Hello, Turkey'?"

I had no clue what she was talking about. I felt sure I never said such a thing. My wife's quizzical look confirmed my doubts. I just replied, "I don't remember saying that. Why do you ask?" That triggered a somewhat-lengthy description of her troubled life but how, through her ups and downs with drugs and lovers leaving her with children, she had a loving grandmother.

She went on to explain, "Gramma was someone who went to church a lot, and she prayed a lot, and I knew she loved me, but I was messed up. Last year my gramma died, but I got to see her before, and I said, 'Gramma, if I ever get back on the right track and you can see me from heaven making good choices, will you somehow tell me "Hello, Turkey"? That's what she always used to call me. Well, this is my second week coming here to church, and this morning I clearly heard you say 'Hello, Turkey.' So I'm thinking I must be on the right track."

Her story struck me, and I told her how much God loved her and said, "Jesus knew what you asked your grandma to say. So He caused you to hear words this morning that I didn't say."

She was dumbfounded. And I was able to introduce her to this Jesus who does remarkable, miraculous things to seek and save the lost—to claim the buried treasures of this world. That's who Jesus is. That's what this parable is about. Our Lord looks at each of us as a treasure, and He will stop at nothing—pay whatever price is necessary—to help you become His possession!

Here's my suggestion: the next time you take Communion, don't think just about how much Jesus paid. Yes, it was His life He gave—it was His body that was broken and His blood that was shed. But consider *why* He paid that price. He wants you to be His. He wants you to no longer be in any kind of bondage to any form of the Enemy's power. Satan has no hold on you. He has no claim on you.

Turns out you are an Etch A Sketch yourself. When you become His, Jesus wonderfully and lovingly turns your life upside down and erases the sin, shame, corruption, and marks the Devil left in your life, granting you a clean slate and heart that He writes on by His Spirit. Because you belong to Him.

20/20 FOCUS

1. This chapter points out that the common interpretation of this parable emphasizes the enormous price a human being must be willing to pay to possess the treasured kingdom of heaven. What difference does it make to see yourself as the treasure Jesus paid to possess, rather than the kingdom being the treasure you must pay to possess?

2. The phrase "and sold all he had" was connected with Philippians 2:6–7, which speaks of the price the Son of God paid to redeem the

world. Can you think of any other Bible verses that speak of His great personal sacrifice?

3. How might things be different in our churches and among Christian believers if the Christus Victor view of salvation was more widely proclaimed and embraced in our time?

4. Take a few moments to pray for a person you would ask Jesus to seek out and save in the miraculous way He claimed the young mom in the "Hello, Turkey" story.

Lord Jesus, I am so thankful You paid the price to reclaim this world … and me. I embrace by faith my freedom from sin and from Satan's hold on me. Help me walk out that freedom in practical ways that show the world I belong to You. Amen.

VISION CHECK

Whenever you begin to think about anything, you start with assumptions you're not even aware of. The key to clear thinking is to release those assumptions. Don't let them control what you see before you check them out like we did in this parable. (Are we right to assume the man who bought the field is a person like ourselves?)

Practice this skill by going to 2 Corinthians 9:15, where Paul wrote, "Thanks be to God for his indescribable gift!" First, identify what most people assume Paul meant by the "indescribable gift" and hold it in question. Then read the preceding verses (vv. 6–14) to see if the common assumption fits the context. Or is the "indescribable gift" referring to something else? Hop on dougnewton.com or the Fresh Eyes app to compare your thoughts with mine.

2

ANOTHER DAY, ANOTHER DENARIUS

The Vineyard Workers

Matthew 20:1–15

What we mean by "fair" and what God
means by "fair" are often different things.

The year our daughters were six and four years old, my wife and I had no money for Christmas presents. We were living on a very low preacher's salary and had been saving all year. By November we had saved about 175 dollars. Then one day we had to dip into our savings and use it up.

For a couple years, we'd sponsored two African refugees who fled to the United States for asylum. When they first came, they didn't know each other. They didn't speak each other's languages and didn't speak English. One was Coptic from Ethiopia, and the other was Muslim from what was then called Zaire (today is the Democratic Republic of Congo). They lived with the four of us. The experience enriched us in every way but financially.

Eventually they learned English well enough to enroll in some basic college courses, get jobs, and move into a very inexpensive apartment. Yosef, the one from Ethiopia, had no car but got a job about ten miles out of town at a clothing factory, so I drove him to work and picked him up every day. It was the only kind of job he could get. Soon he was able to buy a car, a great relief to our family schedule.

Unfortunately, just after Thanksgiving, that car broke down. We had it towed to a nearby service station and found out the repair would cost about—you guessed it—175 dollars. Of course, our hearts sank as we knew what we must do and what it would mean for the kids' Christmas. We got his car fixed.

I honestly don't remember whether we even prayed about the situation, but something wonderful happened. In anticipation of our out-of-state parents coming to our home for Christmas, we wanted to spruce it up a bit. A few months earlier we had bought some living-room wallpaper for a dollar a roll but had not gotten around to hanging it. So early in December we decided to do that. Both of our dads were neatniks and always approached household tasks with excellence, so I knew we needed to do a good job and not cut corners. When the time came to hang the paper on the wall with the fireplace, I had no choice but to take down the mantel so I could run the paper neatly behind it. I didn't want to, but that's what kids do when their dads are perfectionists.

I figured out how the mantel was fastened to the wall and gathered the tools I needed. Just as I disconnected the mantel from the wall, two one-hundred-dollar bills fluttered onto the floor. Sometime before we ever lived in the house, they must have gotten lodged in the crack behind the mantel. Suddenly we had 200 dollars.

But wait. That's not all. A few days later we had a water problem, and I had to slide under the house and crawl on my belly to the back corner. I had never been that far back in the crawl space before and could barely see in the dark. Suddenly I came upon a box. I had no idea what was in it, so I pulled it into the light and found it was an old train set. I thought it might have some value, so I called one of the men in my church who collected model trains to come take a look. Turned out it was rare—rare enough for him to offer us 500 dollars on the spot!

If you're doing the math, our 175-dollar loss was erased by a 700-dollar gain. Not only were we able to give our kids some special gifts, but my wife and I exchanged gifts that year as well. We have no doubt that was an example of God's kindness. But was it a "reward" for our willingness to sacrifice? Is that how the kingdom works? And if so, how much sacrifice is required before you become eligible? And what of other situations where we gave up things we needed but didn't get any divine recompense?

NOT BUSINESS AS USUAL

These kinds of stories and their counterpart (when there's no immediate reward) can lead to confusion. Why does God sometimes cover our expenses (or meet some other concern), while other times we seem to get left hanging? The parable this chapter explores about the landowner and his hired workers adds to that confusion.

As with many of Jesus' parables, He began by saying this is what God's kingdom is like. He wanted us to assume in advance that the kingdom's ways and values will differ from the ways and values of this world, a reality that drives the conflict in this drama. He opened by stating, "For the kingdom of heaven is like a landowner who went out early in the morning to hire workers for his vineyard. He agreed to pay them a denarius for the day and sent them into his vineyard" (Matt. 20:1–2).

Notice how Jesus used language that set up His listeners to process this story according to business values. Words like *hire*, *agreed to pay*, *denarius for the day*, and *sent them* evoke a work-for-hire, verbal contract: "I will pay you X amount of money for X amount of work." The pay was based on the amount each person worked. So the first wave of workers headed off to work first thing in the morning. Jesus continued: "About nine in the morning he went out and saw others standing in the marketplace doing nothing. He told them, 'You also go and work in my vineyard, and I will pay you whatever is right.' So they went" (vv. 3–5).

Notice that the landowner did not specify the amount of pay. The workers simply took the landowner's word that he would do "whatever is right." Jesus left His listeners nodding, recognizing a familiar situation: the owner would calculate what the workers' pay would be based on the one-denarius benchmark promised to the early-morning workers. It would be a simple calculation even people who weren't CPAs could figure out easily: their pay would be in the neighborhood of one denarius minus one-fourth of a denarius, because they would have worked three fewer hours than the early hires (three out of a total of twelve work hours equals one-fourth of the day). Clearly, that would be "right."

Jesus added the repetition of traditional storytelling: "He went out again about noon and about three in the afternoon and did the same thing" (v. 5).

It went without saying that the owner would also treat them fairly. The workers who began at noon, the sixth hour of the workday, would receive one denarius minus six-twelfths of a denarius, or a half denarius, because they would have worked half as long as the early workers. The pay of the workers who began at three would be similarly calculated.

With the pattern firmly embedded in His listeners' minds, Jesus continued: "About five in the afternoon he went out and found still others standing around. He asked them, 'Why have you been standing here all day long doing nothing?' 'Because no one has hired us,' they answered. He said to them, 'You also go and work in my vineyard'" (vv. 6–7).

At this point, some of Jesus' listeners might have begun to cock their heads with a question niggling their minds: Why would the landowner even bother to hire workers for only one hour's work? But they probably just passed it off as an oddity of the story, until suddenly the whole situation took an unexpected turn: "When evening came, the owner of the vineyard said to his foreman, 'Call the workers and pay them their wages, beginning with the last ones hired and going on to the first'" (v. 8).

This is very interesting. The story makes it clear that none of the workers knew what the others would earn at the end of the day. Only the earliest workers knew what their pay would be—one denarius. As the parable proceeds, the landowner pays everyone the same amount of money—one denarius. That in itself shocks everyone's worldly senses. Not only does the landowner's pay scale violate good business practice, but his decision to let the early workers know what he was giving everyone else—especially the one-hour workers—also violates common sense. If you know the full-day workers will be mad, pay them first and send them home so they don't see what you're giving the others!

Clearly, the landowner in the story—and remember, this whole parable reveals what God's kingdom is like—intended everyone to be confronted by a shocking set of values. Through this, Jesus, the storyteller, was about to reveal the values of the kingdom of heaven—His kingdom. The landowner gave everyone the same amount for some reason. And the rest of the parable expresses the clash between the kingdom of heaven and the kingdom of this world:

So when those came who were hired first, they expected to receive more. But each one of them also received a denarius. When they received it, they began to grumble against the landowner. "These who were hired last worked only one hour," they said, "and you have made them equal to us who have borne the burden of the work and the heat of the day."

But he answered one of them, "I am not being unfair to you, friend. Didn't you agree to work for a denarius? Take your pay and go. I want to give the one who was hired last the same as I gave you. Don't I have the right to do what I want with my own money? Or are you envious because I am generous?" (vv. 10–15)

Notice that Jesus never had the landowner explain his reasoning. He simply made him sound like the stereotypical parent who doesn't want to explain himself to the kids: "Because I said so." It is left up to us to sort this out. The landowner promised all the workers who began later that he would give them whatever was right. How in the world … er, how in heaven … can it be right to give them the same amount?

DAYWORK AND DAILY BREAD

Believe it or not, Jesus' original listeners might have found answering that question easier than we do today, because they understood something we can't know without a little research. Here are two things you must know to discover the good news in this parable: What are hired workers, and what is a denarius?

A quick look at footnotes in a study Bible or basic commentary reveals that hired workers were day laborers. They had no guarantee of regular employment but gathered with a group of other laborers every day in hopes of being hired for a day's work in the fields. And a denarius was the equivalent of a day's wage.

This still occurs in our time in hundreds of towns and cities around the country where day laborers wait to be hired for farm or construction work. Understand, if a day laborer doesn't work, his family doesn't eat. It was and still is that simple. If you are a dayworker, you can do nothing to control whether you get hired, except to be available and wait for a truck to drive up and for the driver to tell you to hop in. That's why the dialogue between the owner and the workers emphasizes they were "standing around" not out of laziness but simply because no one had come by: "About five in the afternoon he went out and found still others standing around. He asked them, 'Why have you been standing here all day long doing nothing?' 'Because no one has hired us,' they answered" (Matt. 20:6–7).

In this parable—and all Jesus' listeners would have known this—the workers' only hope for meeting their daily needs was for a landowner to come along and invite them to work. The reaction of the laborers who had worked all day makes sense to us. They worked longer, so they should have gotten more money. But this parable is about the values of the kingdom—it begins with "the kingdom of heaven is like"—not the values of the world. The landowner's calculations were based not on the number of hours worked but on typical daily needs. All dayworkers' needs are the same. The ones who didn't have the opportunity to work all day still needed a full day's pay. The kingdom of heaven is not about getting someone's sweat but about giving someone bread. That's good news, but the news gets even better.

THE OWNER'S PRIORITY

Based on the parable's pattern, what would the owner give a person invited to work at 5:30 p.m.? Or 5:45? That's right: a denarius. Why? Because the landowner's concern was giving all the workers what they needed for the day.

The vital question is, Why was the landowner looking for unhired workers at the last hour of the day? What good would they do him then? Clearly, the reason is not about how much labor the landowner needed done but about how much support people needed to make it through the day. The owner desired to give all the workers a chance to get what they needed. He wanted no one left without a chance, so much so that he kept looking for people long after they were useful to him.

At 5:59, the master could say, "Come get in the truck," and he'd pay that laborer for a full day too. That's what is *right* in this kingdom. Even at 5:59:59, if a laborer had done nothing but lift his leg to hop in the truck as the six o'clock whistle blew, he'd get a full day's wage! Isn't that the kind of landowner you really want to work for?

I can't tell you why my wife and I suddenly discovered 700 dollars after having given up our kids' Christmas gifts money. Was it a reward for doing something nice? Perhaps. We make no claims. What we know is that God does reward, but He is also generous in ways that go beyond anything we have earned and gets to be generous whenever and however He wants. And this parable in particular shows His passion to invite anyone and everyone to join His work, and He will give us what we need to make it through every day.

20/20 FOCUS

Two goals of this book are to stir your heart with richer insights into God's heart and to inspire stronger compassion for the needs of people. With that in mind ...

1. Imagine being your family's sole wage earner but not knowing from one day to the next whether you will have work. Imagine the hours ticking by—nine o'clock, twelve o'clock, then three o'clock—and still having no opportunity to earn any money. What could you do? How would you feel? And what if it were like that many days out of every month?

2. Take a few moments to do an online search of "day laborers" or "National Day Labor Study" to get an idea of the number and plight of people in America who are in the very position you imagined in question 1.

3. Think about what you discovered in your research and reflect again on this parable's focus on God's compassionate heart. How is the Holy Spirit stirring your heart?

4. Think beyond the daily need for money and food. What other "basics" for daily life and stable living do most people need? Do you think this parable can be extended to speak to the Lord's concern for those needs as well? Are there any Scripture passages that support that extension?

Lord Jesus, this parable's view of Your grace and compassion grips my heart, first with gratitude and then with conviction. Help me live in confidence regarding Your provision for me and my family. But also help me find ways to imitate Your dedicated compassion for the daily needs of others. Amen.

VISION CHECK

Stories often have a trajectory that increases or decreases the action, circumstances, or ideas to encourage us to ask, "What might happen if we go one step beyond where the story leaves off?" In this chapter, we followed the trajectory and imagined what might happen if the master hired a worker the very last minute of the workday. This technique often results in seeing some point with more impact or clarity.

Practice this technique on Gideon's story in Judges 7. Notice the trajectory of the decreasing size of his army as they were about to go into battle against 135,000 Midianites. Then take one or more steps along that trajectory and see where your mind goes. Compare your thoughts with mine on dougnewton.com or the Fresh Eyes app.

3

WHERE SHOULD THE EMPHASIS GO?

The Lost Son

Luke 15:11–32

Who's the most important character
in the parable of the prodigal son?

English is among the most difficult languages to learn for people raised in a non-English-speaking country. The language seems to have no rules, except that there are exceptions to every rule. Even rules about exceptions have exceptions—"*I* before *E* except after *C*," but what about *height, feign, reign,* or *rein?* Maybe it's *I* before *E* except after *C* and *H* and *F* and *R*. But then there's *worrier* and *healthier*. Maybe our highly prized independence caused the English language to run amok.

On top of spelling, there's no rhyme or reason to pronunciation. People who try to learn English as a second language must remember not only the meaning and the spelling but also the sound of every word, which is vital for communication. This struck me quite powerfully when a good friend from another country said recently, "This is a terri-BULL DEVIL-opment."

It took me a minute to realize he wasn't trying to say something about a "bull-devil." He was, as they say, placing the em-PHA-sis on the wrong syl-LA-ble.

A similar thing has happened to Jesus' parables. Sometimes we miss the very point Jesus wanted to emphasize. The parable of the lost son, often called the parable of the prodigal son, is a case in point.

It is arguably the most famous of all the parables, the Good Samaritan its nearest rival. Undoubtedly, it's hope-filled and even life-changing, depicting God's immense love and mercy like no other story or passage in Scripture. But it reveals something else that's often missed.

THREE CHARACTERS, THREE CHOICES

The parable of the prodigal son is so revered it's nearly impossible to reframe. It's also nearly impossible to exaggerate the three main characters. There's the younger son's disgraceful premature demand of his inheritance, as if he said to his father, "I wish you were already dead." There's also his stupefying self-indulgence that led to his descent into absolute poverty. Even the desperate, self-serving nature of his motive for seeking reconciliation with his father can't be overstated.

The older son's arrogance and coldness toward his brother kindles scornful boos and hisses. His ingratitude and rejection of the grace he's always enjoyed from his father appalls us.

As for the father, some Christian writers have pointed out that since *prodigal* comes from the same root as *prodigious*, the parable could properly be renamed the prodigal father because of his overflowing love. Who hasn't been moved by the image of the father running to welcome his wandering child? What wanderer hasn't been thrilled to imagine those forgiving arms? The celebration over our return from our wanderings outstrips even the most extravagant dream of Christmas trees surrounded with presents and parties thrown just for us.

Applications are myriad and adjust to the need. For wandering and broken people, we emphasize the father's open arms. For dealing with judgment, we look at the older brother. For those tempted by self-indulgence, we unpack the consequences of wasteful spending and wild extravagance. It's as though we hear three syllables and our circumstances determine which to emphasize.

Which character do you think is the protagonist—the younger son, the father, or the older son? Or is it two of them? All three? After all, we know it's important to get the EM-pha-sis on the right SYL-la-ble.

THE OTHER CHARACTER

The best answer, I believe, is "None of the above." Jesus had another character in mind not named in this parable but established earlier in the chapter. For any parable, we always look back for what situation, question, or comment set it up. When we do that here, we discover this parable is the last of three Jesus told in rapid sequence. All of them focus on something lost that was found: a lost sheep, a lost coin, and a lost son. To help Bible readers see that continuity, the NIV translation appropriately titles this parable "Lost Son" rather than the more traditional "Prodigal Son."

All three parables tie together thematically, so the "lost son" parable is the culmination of Jesus' response to whatever triggered the first two parables. Luke made it very clear: "Now the tax collectors and sinners were all gathering around to hear Jesus. But the Pharisees and the teachers of the law muttered, 'This man welcomes sinners and eats with them.' Then Jesus told them this parable ..." (Luke 15:1–3).

Jesus' welcoming attitude toward the unrighteous "riffraff" disturbed the Pharisees and the teachers of the law. But, of course, Jesus did not see the "riffraff" that way. They were lost people hungering for rescue and hope. So Jesus starkly contrasted the Pharisees' bad attitude with His attitude. However, His attitude was not just His. It was the attitude of heaven itself. You can tell how important this issue was to Jesus because He didn't tell just one parable to make His point. He told three in succession.

The first parable tells about the joy of the owner of one hundred sheep who left his flock to search diligently for one lost sheep. Jesus expected His listeners to identify with the shepherd's concern and eventual happiness. "Suppose one of you has a hundred sheep and loses one of them. Doesn't he leave the ninety-nine in the open country and go after the lost sheep until he finds it? And when he finds it, he joyfully puts it on his shoulders and goes home" (vv. 4–6).

Jesus told how the shepherd's joy spilled over into celebration with his friends and neighbors. "Then he calls his friends and neighbors together and says, 'Rejoice with me; I have found my lost sheep'" (v. 6). However, simply reporting the shepherd's joy was not His main point. Jesus wanted His listeners to imagine the shepherd's joy and multiply that to get an approximation of the degree of joy in heaven when one lost sinner is found and repents. Jesus directly said, "I tell you that in the same way there will be more rejoicing in heaven over one sinner who repents than over ninety-nine righteous persons who do not need to repent" (v. 7).

The second parable is almost identical, except it focuses on the efforts of a woman who owned ten coins to find one she lost. Her joy over recovering the lost coin drove her, like the shepherd, to share that joy with friends and neighbors. And again, Jesus made the point about immense joy in heaven triggered by one lost sinner who is found and repents. "In the same way, I tell you, there is rejoicing in the presence of the angels of God over one sinner who repents" (v. 10).

In other words, Jesus' purpose in telling these parables was to reveal the contrast between the Pharisees' attitude and heaven's. He was not just talking about a shepherd and a lost sheep; a woman and a lost coin; or a father, an older brother, and a lost son. The main character in these stories is *heaven*, and the focus was—and is—on heaven's reactions.

ACTUAL AND IMPERISHABLE

Finally, Jesus artfully increased the emotional impact of His stories when He told the third parable, by talking not of a lost sheep or coin but of a lost child. He dramatically detailed the lost person's desperation and allowed His listeners time to feel the father's pain. But the parable still retains the same structure: something lost, something found, tremendous joy spills over into celebration.

The one thing missing in this parable is an explicit statement about the joy happening in heaven. That's because it is not needed. Jesus mentioned a party that hints at celestial celebration (we'll get to that momentarily), but heaven wasn't specifically mentioned. Jesus had already established the literary pattern in the first two parables, leaving the listener able to make the necessary connection.

Then Jesus brought the polemical purpose of the three parables home. He turned to the matter of the older son's attitude, which mirrored the Pharisees' bad attitude. Jesus said, "The older brother became angry and refused to go in. So his father went out and pleaded with him. But he answered his father, 'Look! All these years I've been slaving for you and never disobeyed your orders. Yet you never gave me even a young goat so I could celebrate with my friends. But when this son of yours who has squandered your property with prostitutes comes home, you kill the fattened calf for him!'" (Luke 15:28–30).

Even though we might like to bask in the father's love as the parable's emphatic point, Jesus clearly combined the three parables into one strong rebuke of the Pharisees' attitude. However, remember the literary structure of the first two parables, which end with a glimpse into heaven. Even though Jesus concluded this parable with the older son's scornful attitude, we must remember Jesus' emphasis in this chapter: the utter contrast between what was going on in the Pharisees' hearts and what goes on in the heart of heaven. And even though we can draw heart-warming lessons from other elements in the parable, the structural and thematic connection between all three parables compels us to interpret the earthly father's celebration as a limited but accurate picture of what goes on in heaven when a lost and wandering child is found. That was the main focus, rather than the father's love. Jesus stated, "But the father said to his servants, 'Quick! Bring the best robe and put it on him. Put a ring on his finger and sandals on his feet. Bring the fattened calf and kill it. Let's have a feast and celebrate'" (vv. 22–23).

Scholars often recognize that the robe, ring, sandals, and fattened calf all have symbolic meanings. But the parable's full impact comes from understanding that Jesus intended more than symbolism. From the moment a person comes home to God through repentance, he or she is adorned with the "best robe" of righteousness and honor. This takes place in heaven. It doesn't matter how inadequate, incomplete, or undeserving we may still be. Our righteousness and right to take a place of honor and acceptance before the Father are complete.

In that very moment, we also receive the signet ring of the Father's authority. A signet ring confirms one's authority to act and can be used either by the one who holds power or by someone else on behalf of the one holding power. In Christ that authority has been conferred in heaven, allowing us to act on God's behalf here on earth. Nothing more needs to be learned or earned in order to take action in God's name, whether in prayer or service. Because that authority has been given in heaven, we can "approach God's throne of grace with confidence" (Heb. 4:16) and join our Lord in His ongoing ministry of intercession (Eph. 2:6; Rom. 8:34; Heb. 7:25).

Similarly, the sandals and the fattened calf symbolize wealth, position, and honor. But these are not mere symbols; they represent heaven's reality. As Paul wrote, we have been "blessed … in the heavenly realms with every spiritual blessing in Christ" (Eph. 1:3). God's work in you on earth is always the outgrowth of work already accomplished in God's eternal realm represented by the word *heaven*. That's why Peter explained: "Praise be to the God and Father of our Lord Jesus Christ! In his great mercy he has given us new birth into a living hope through the resurrection of Jesus Christ from the dead, and into an inheritance that can never perish, spoil or fade. This inheritance is kept in heaven for you" (1 Pet. 1:3–4).

I grew up in a denomination that heavily emphasized free will—that is, the importance of a human being choosing to repent and trust Jesus Christ for salvation. I still believe that, but in my years of ministry I have discovered the downside to that emphasis: spiritual insecurity. When people think their choice saved them, they inevitably worry about whether their ongoing choices are enough to keep them saved.

I once spoke with a pastor of a large church in a retirement community. He told me how sad he was that many of the wonderful senior saints in his congregation became more and more nervous about their eternal destiny as they anticipated the approach of death. "What if in my final hours I have bad thoughts?" they wondered. "What if I blurt out something horrible in my pain? What if I haven't been faithful enough to the Lord?"

I hear similar questions from Christians of every age group when they don't grasp what happened in heaven for them on the day they repented or what is being "kept in heaven" for those "who through faith are shielded by God's power until the coming of the salvation that is ready to be revealed in the last time" (vv. 4–5). They live in fear of God's presumed frustration with them over their shortcomings and besetting sins. They do not know how to counteract the condemning barbs of the Enemy of our souls, who is called the *accuser*. They don't experience freedom through the truths that set them free, because they assume their relationship with God depends on their ongoing choices.

Don't get me wrong; our choices on earth are important. Young sons can always leave home a second time. The early church acknowledged the possibility of apostasy (i.e., willfully renouncing Jesus as Lord). But that is a far cry from the case of sincere Christians who love the Lord but often struggle to obey. Our position in God's family will feel so much more firm and secure when we understand that position has been sealed in heaven, as this parable portrays, and does not depend on our weak wills and shifting passions.

Heaven. That's the main character in all three parables. What's happening there is the most important thing Jesus wanted us to see. So yes, there are things happening on earth, but there are greater things going on in heaven. There's human choice, but there's God's grace. We simply must learn to keep the emphasis on the right syllable.

20/20 FOCUS

1. In this chapter, we thought of heaven as a "character" because Jesus focused on the joyful behavior of angels in heaven. Can you name other behaviors Scripture attributes to heaven?

2. This chapter's core argument is: since Jesus' first two parables give glimpses of actual events in heaven, we should understand the father's reaction in the third parable as revealing actual events occurring in heaven as well. What difference does it make to you to see these reactions as representing real events?

3. The Pharisees' grumbling attitude about Jesus' kindness toward sinners triggered His emphatic telling of three parables in rapid succession. He must want us to be very careful to avoid that attitude. What category of "sinners" are you inclined to grumble about?

Lord Jesus, it helps me tremendously to know that my inheritance of righteousness and my royal identity are being "kept in heaven" for me. I never want to forget that and slip into fear. I also never want to take that for granted and become lackadaisical in my hunger for holiness. Help me live in the joy of Your gracious love and acceptance, even as I extend that grace to others who have yet to come home to You. Amen.

VISION CHECK

You never fully understand what's going on in a person's mind until you know what triggered what he or she did or said. You have to ask, "I know what you said, but why did you say it? What are you getting at?"

One day Jesus famously told His disciples, "With God all things are possible" (Matt. 19:26). We like to quote that in general terms—and rightly so. But what triggered that statement? And does that knowledge trigger any new insights in you? Write down those discoveries and compare them with mine on dougnewton.com or the Fresh Eyes app.

WHEN YOUR CUPBOARDS ARE BARE

The Friend in Need

Luke 11:5–9

What do you say when you
have nothing to say?

I hadn't even finished unloading our moving van when my first emergency call came as the ridiculously young, first-time pastor of a Bowling Green, Kentucky, church. A teenager from the church had crashed into a tree and severed his spinal cord. I quickly wiped away my sweat, changed shirts, and hopped into the car to race to a nearby hospital to see the distraught family. I had no clue what I would say. I had not yet been to seminary. I barely knew how to get to the hospital.

When I arrived and found the family in the intensive care waiting room, I learned Peter was conscious, and the family invited me to go in by myself and talk to him—a person I had never met. A situation I had never faced. I had no clue what I would say.

When I opened the door to one of the first hospital rooms I had entered in my twenty-four years of sheltered life, I saw him suspended from a contraption that resembled a large hamster wheel more than a bed. Peter was laid out prone about three feet off the ground, facedown. Pins drilled into both of his temples were attached to a metal halo and to cables that held him taut. A mirror lay on the floor so he could see who was talking to him. But I chose to ignore the mirror and slid underneath him on my back so I could look up into his frightened eyes face-to-face.

But still I had no clue what I would say ...

That was my introduction to a life of ministry during which I have found myself in that very position, at least symbolically, many times: flat on my back, gazing into frightened eyes, with no clue what to say. Yet more often than not, something remarkable happens that has a lot to do with this parable and its famous concluding verse: "Ask and it will be given to you; seek and you will find; knock and the door will be opened to you" (Luke 11:9).

In order to gain the hope offered in these twenty-two words, we need to examine grammatically the parable Jesus shared just before stating them. Without a clear look at the context, we won't grasp the very specific way in which Jesus intended us to hear this promise about asking and receiving. In this case, our "fresh eyes" approach is a matter of narrowing the application rather than expanding it.

IDENTIFYING ANTECEDENTS

This parable is the story of a man who approached a friend at midnight for some much-needed food. The secret to a fresh insight into this parable is found, surprisingly, in the bevy of pronouns that are detached from their antecedents.

Maybe a quick grammar lesson is in order. Join me back in your sixth-grade classroom. A noun is a word that refers to a person, place, or thing. Sound familiar? A pronoun is a word that refers to some previously stated noun, called the antecedent. So, for example, you can't use the little pronoun *it* until you have named the object *it* refers to. Otherwise no one will know what "it" you're talking about. The world is full of "its" galore. If you're first talking about a car and then you use the word *it*, everyone knows you're talking about the car. Similarly, you should use *he* or *she* only after you've named the he or she.

The problem with the brief story of the midnight food request is that there are more pronouns running around than school kids at recess. However, the good news is that if we diligently identify the antecedent behind every pronoun, the story becomes much more focused and Jesus' famous twenty-two-word saying becomes much more powerful.

First take a moment to read the story in the New International Version (Luke 11:5–8) and notice all the italicized pronouns.

> Then Jesus said to *them*, "Suppose *you* have a
> friend, and *you* go to *him* at midnight and say,
> 'Friend, lend *me* three loaves of bread; a friend

of *mine* on a journey has come to *me*, and *I* have no food to offer *him*.' And suppose the *one* inside answers, 'Don't bother *me*. The door is already locked, and *my* children and *I* are in bed. *I* can't get up and give *you* anything.' *I* tell *you*, even though *he* will not get up and give *you* the bread because of friendship, yet because of *your* shameless audacity *he* will surely get up and give *you* as much as *you* need."

See what I mean? There's not a single named person in the story! It contains a mishmash of pronouns. Our task becomes to identify the cast of characters in these four verses. We'll assign some contemporary names, since none is given.

Cast of Characters

Jesus	The one telling the story
The disciples	The ones hearing the story
Sam/you	The one who goes next door to get food
Fred	The one Sam goes to at midnight
George	The one who visits Sam and needs food

Then *Jesus* said to *the disciples*, "Suppose *Sam* has a friend, and *Sam* goes to *Fred* at midnight and says, '*Fred*, lend *me* three loaves of bread; *George*, a friend of *mine* on a journey, has

come to *me*, and *I* have no food to offer *him*.'
And suppose *Fred* answers, 'Don't bother *me*.
The door is already locked, and *my* children
and *I* are in bed. *I* can't get up and give *you*
anything.' *I* tell *you*, even though *Fred* will
not get up and give *Sam* the bread because
of friendship, yet because of *Sam's* shameless
audacity *Fred* will surely get up and give *Sam*
as much as *Sam* needs.

SHARPENING THE POINT

First, why did Sam go to Fred's house? To ask for three loaves of
bread. Why did Sam need bread? Because Sam needed to feed
George, who, while on a journey, had come to Sam's home. But
why did Sam need to ask Fred for bread? Because Sam had no
bread. Let's go deeper.

Why did Sam go to Fred at midnight? Maybe George
showed up late and was not hungry in just the ordinary sense.
He may have been in very rough shape. So famished, in fact,
that Sam considered it an emergency.

Wouldn't it take a serious problem for you to disturb one
of your friends in the middle of the night? You and your friend
have to get up in the morning to go to work—and you'll wake
the friend's kids! Thanks a lot, Sam!

Step back now and summarize this situation in its context. The disciples started off this chapter asking Jesus to teach them to pray. He gave them a prayer template we call the Lord's Prayer, which guides us to seek daily bread. "He said to them, 'When you pray, say: 'Father, hallowed be your name, your kingdom come. Give us each day our daily bread'" (Luke 11:2–3).

So Jesus had just established that prayer, at least in part, is about trusting God for daily bread. Then Jesus launched into this brief story. A story about one of the disciples being in a situation where he needs daily bread. But it's not for himself. It's for a person in desperate need, and the disciple has nothing to offer. He goes through every cupboard in the house, looking for something. Bread. Ramen noodles. Twinkies. Something to help his famished friend in desperate need. But there's nothing. Empty cupboards.

After describing this desperate need, Jesus segued from story to promise: "So I say to you: Ask … seek … knock and the door will be opened to you" (v. 9). Suddenly these words, too often heard only as a broad generality, compress into a diamond-like promise with one brilliant setting: it's for people who find themselves with absolutely nothing to offer when facing a person in desperate need.

And even more particularly, it's about needing life-giving bread, which so often symbolizes divine words. Words of life. Words that feed the soul. Words that bring peace. Words that give divine counsel. Words that offer hope. But words you don't have.

FINDING DIVINE WORDS

One day about three years ago, a fellow pastor from another city asked to see me. He came to my office and poured out his frustrations over years of pastoral ministry fraught with one disappointment after another. He was wired to be a change agent but had been serving in a series of status-quo churches that seemed unresponsive.

The constant turmoil and resulting self-doubt brought him to the point of throwing in the towel. "I can't take it anymore," he said. The sense of defeat seemed to weaken his voice. His spirit lacked strength enough to hold up his head.

While my heart went out to him, I could not identify. Perhaps I have been spoiled by relatively conflict-free pastorates. While I've faced my share of challenges that sapped my strength for a season, I had never been close to clerical suicide. I didn't know what to say that would help. The cupboards of my own experience were empty. Plus, I had never talked with any other pastors who had survived such a season. That cupboard was empty too. I had no bread of counsel or hope to offer. And I certainly wasn't about to mouth the obvious platitudes: "Just hang in there. It will get better. You're just going through a discouraging time. The Lord will lift you up." Moldy bread is worse than no bread.

What did I do? I trusted Jesus' promise for receiving divinely supplied bread for desperate people in the context of prayer. So even though no words of wisdom came to mind, I asked to pray for him before he left.

I got up from my chair, walked over behind him, laid both hands on his shoulders, and prayed blessing from one brother to another. I had hardly finished one sentence before a scene came to my mind. It wasn't a vision; it was more like a description that arrived with a surge of energy. I spoke it out loud: "Lord, my brother feels like a palm tree at the edge of the ocean. Gale-force winds are blasting against him, and he feels like he's about to be blown over. But he has been standing strong, and I thank You that he will continue to stand strong against those winds and continue to bring glory to You."

Within just a couple more sentences the winds of that prayer died down and I concluded. I wondered if my friend had sensed the surge of passion that I had, so I asked.

He said, "I can't believe what you just prayed! Before I left home this morning to come see you, I told my wife almost those exact words. I said, 'I feel like a palm tree at the edge of the ocean with gale-force winds coming against me, and I'm about to be blown over.' But because you prayed those same words, I know the Lord is telling me He is pleased with me and that I will keep standing."

He left fed. His starvation ended. God provided bread from heaven's cupboards that I didn't have. My colleague continues to pastor faithfully and serves with stability and strength among his people and in his community. And I believe I experienced what is available to all of us, according to the apostle Paul: "Let the message of Christ dwell among you richly as you teach and admonish one another with all wisdom" (Col. 3:16).

This "message [word] of Christ" dwelling richly in us is not only a matter of quoting Bible verses. Often, it's a matter of having just the right *awareness* by seeing into the spiritual realm. This awareness forms ideas, images, and words that fit what's really going on, and at just the right moment. It's experiencing what our Lord Jesus experienced that led Him to say, "For I did not speak on my own, but the Father who sent me commanded me to say all that I have spoken.… So whatever I say is just what the Father has told me to say" (John 12:49–50).

Sometimes when we are confronted with desperate needs, it is necessary to seek the assistance of trained counselors and caregivers. But many Christians never experience the fulfillment of the Lord's promise to provide life-giving words, because they find their cupboards of knowledge, experience, or giftedness bare and pass people off too quickly to "someone else more qualified." Our bare cupboards become a barrier. But if we would let our bare cupboards become a signal to ask, seek, and knock, we would often find bread—daily bread— for others who need our help.

Every time you face a situation and feel inadequate—*I've never faced someone in this situation before. I have no clue what to say. I haven't been trained to handle this. I've never been through what he's going through*—that's exactly the time *not* to back away. Go ask. Go seek. Go knock. And you will receive the bread you need for others.

As I crawled under Peter's suspended body and looked up into his eyes, I found words flowing from my heart that brought the sense of God's peace to a person whose limbs would never feel again. In this case, as in most cases since, they weren't miraculous words of divine knowledge—I don't even remember what I said. But they flowed easily and with gentle confidence. The flicker of hope I saw in his eyes in that room dimmed by silent fear gave me confidence divine comfort had come through my simple words. That moment I determined I would never run from situations when my cupboards are bare.

20/20 FOCUS

1. Think of a couple of times when you faced a challenging situation and didn't know what to say. What was it like? Did you finally say something?

2. Are you inclined to assume you have nothing to say if you aren't trained or experienced to handle certain kinds of problems? Do you

tend to dismiss the advice of others if they have never gone through what you're going through?

3. It is often said that when friends face rough times you don't have to say anything; your presence with them is enough. But is that always true, or is it sometimes a cop-out? What if we only ever had God's presence but not His voice? What might we be missing?

4. Think of a person to whom you have hesitated to speak because you don't know what to say. How about reconsidering and applying Jesus' ask-seek-knock promise to that situation and seeing what happens?

Lord Jesus, I'm sure You understand how awkward and incapable I often feel when someone needs my help and guidance but I don't know what to say. I don't want to say anything stupid, insensitive, or incorrect. But I also admit these fears often keep me silent. The next time help me pause and pray according to the ask-seek-knock promise before I assume I shouldn't speak. Amen.

VISION CHECK

When studying a difficult passage, it often helps to replace every pronoun with its antecedent and then read the passage aloud. It may sound awkward or repetitious, but you will find the point becomes either clearer or more emphatic.

Try doing that with Luke 6:35: "Love your enemies, do good to them, and lend to them without expecting to get anything back."

There are only two pronouns to replace, but when you do your heart should be struck with new and challenging thoughts. If you want a double whammy, read the preceding context starting with verse 27 and notice how Jesus wants us to respond to other categories of people who could be considered enemies. Then get on dougnewton.com or the Fresh Eyes app and compare your thoughts with mine.

5

BEFORE YOU CAST STONES

The Unmerciful Servant
Matthew 18:23–35

Go ahead and be appalled, but
then look in the mirror.

I set a thirty-five-acre field on fire when I was eight years old. It was an accident. But like most of my "accidents," it showcased my stupidity and sinful nature.

I was at my neighbors' house, playing in the basement with their two kids who were a couple years younger than I. A matchbook in an ashtray on an end table caught my attention. My parents didn't smoke, so we didn't have matches lying around to ignite a kid's curiosity. I could not resist this novel temptation—to have matches!—so I snatched and stuffed them in my pocket when the other kids weren't looking.

Then my as-yet-untamed ego had a brilliant idea: I could be the big kid. The one who impresses the little kids. I suggested we go outside, where I would show them something "cool." We walked a quarter mile down the road and out into someone's field—I didn't know whose—and I led the little kids behind some bushes where we couldn't be seen.

"C'mere," I said, then showed them the matchbook. "Wanna see me start a little fire?" They didn't seem quite as interested as I'd imagined, but still, they joined me as I stooped down, scooped together some twigs and dry grass, and struck a match. The wind blew it out.

That should have been my first warning not to light a fire. But of course I was too young and cocky and stupid for that thought to spring to mind. So I struck a second match, and this time it ignited the brush I had gathered.

I stepped back like a magician with a voilà gesture that lasted barely two seconds before the fire started to spread. Fast! I tried stomping it out, but the flames ate up the dry grass too quickly in all directions. The only reasonable thing to do—reasonable to an eight-year-old boy about to get into big trouble, that is—was to run! I think the two little kids ran too, but I was no longer thinking about them or their adulation. I did not look back.

Just before I got home, I stopped running in case my mom was outside. She wasn't, so I lingered in the yard for a little while and tried to divert my worry by climbing a tree or two. I pretended I didn't hear the fire siren but climbed a little higher to see the smoke as I worked on my alibi. Eventually, I scrambled down to go into the house and walked with forced nonchalance into the kitchen past my mom, who was sitting at the table— "Hi, Mom"—and immediately up to my room. At least that's where I was headed when she called me back.

"Doug, do you know anything about a fire out in the Andersons' field?"

"A fire?"

"The Andersons said they thought you were out there with a couple other kids."

"Oh yeah, a fire." It's amazing how fast the human mind can produce lies. By the time I was eight, I was already very quick—albeit not very good—at it. "Yeah, Jimmy and Carrie and I were out there, and I saw somebody had started a fire. I tried to put it out, but I couldn't," I said.

"Somebody else started the fire?" Mom looked me in the eyes. Hers were red and moist now.

"Yeah, but I don't know who. Probably one of the big kids around here was smoking or something."

"Well, Mrs. Collier called me and said a matchbook was missing from her ashtray in the basement."

"Really? They have ashtrays down there? Do they smoke? I guess they aren't Christians, are they?" I hoped my budding legalism would distract my mother.

"Doug, tell me the truth. Actually, let's just go down to the Andersons together and tell them the truth."

That was the longest walk of my young life as my mom marched me down to face two soot-stained people who had just finished fighting a fire that burned thirty acres of their land. I confessed. They did the right thing and did not try to make me feel better. They let shame smolder in hopes of making sorrow burn and the lesson last a lifetime.

The memory of that long walk serves as a metaphor to me of how hard it is for me and most people to face the truth about ourselves and accept blame. Even when we know we're wrong, we still attempt to stifle our consciences with excuses, which leads me to a fresh way of looking at the familiar parable of the unmerciful servant.

APPALLING BEHAVIOR

Jesus told this parable in response to Peter's question about how many times we must be willing to forgive a person. Peter wondered if the expectation was upward of seven times. Jesus responded with "seventy-seven times" (or "seventy times seven," depending on your translation) and then told a parable about a debtor who owed his master millions of dollars.

After the man pleaded with his master to show mercy and not sell his whole family into slavery to repay the debt, the master canceled it entirely and let him go. However, almost immediately the forgiven man went out and found someone who owed him a couple bucks, and, in an atrocious display of mercilessness, the former debtor … Well, just read the text: "But when that servant went out, he found one of his fellow servants who owed him a hundred silver coins. He grabbed him and began to choke him. 'Pay back what you owe me!' he demanded. His fellow servant fell to his knees and begged him, 'Be patient with me, and I will pay it back.' But he refused.

Instead, he went off and had the man thrown into prison until he could pay the debt" (Matt. 18:28–30).

It's hard to imagine how anyone could be so callous! How could someone who had been forgiven millions be so unforgiving over a couple bucks? In the parable, that was also the reaction of an audience of fellow servants who couldn't believe their eyes when they witnessed the event. Jesus said, "When the other servants saw what had happened, they were outraged and went and told their master everything that had happened" (v. 31).

Jesus knew that anyone witnessing such an act of injustice, or hearing about it, would share the fellow servants' point of view. So He crafted the story to place us among that audience of witnesses. We cheer their act of whistle-blowing. We would have done the same thing, and the momentum of this story rushes us toward a satisfying resolution. "Then the master called the servant in. 'You wicked servant,' he said, 'I canceled all that debt of yours because you begged me to. Shouldn't you have had mercy on your fellow servant just as I had on you?' In anger his master handed him over to the jailers to be tortured, until he should pay back all he owed" (vv. 32–34).

We cheer again. As part of the horrified onlookers, we are thrilled by how quickly the unmerciful servant had his forgiveness rescinded and his unpayable debt reinstated. Justice is wonderfully sweet.

However, the parable's pace causes us to speed right past a moment that should be given more attention. A "fresh eyes" look at a Scripture text sometimes requires slowing down and not jumping so quickly from sentence to sentence or scene to scene without wondering what might have happened in between. This parable is a case in point. Between the cancellation of the servant's debt and the time he started demanding his money from a fellow servant, a moment must have come when the unmerciful servant thought about what his fellow servant owed him.

REASONABLE RATIONALIZATIONS

Reasonably, we might ask, "What was he thinking in that moment when he decided to go after repayment from his fellow servant so mercilessly?" Unless this man was a total sociopath, he must have had reasons he thought justified his action, either before or after the fact. To be sure, the parable does not attempt to expose those reasons. Probably because they don't matter to the master. In effect, the parable allows no excuse for such behavior, because it does not grant the servant an opportunity to explain it. But that doesn't mean the unmerciful servant did not have one or two or more excuses. What might they have been? And why meditate on that?

Simply put, we might be capable of similar rationalization and self-justification. Taking a cue from Jesus' words to the adulterous woman's accusers (John 8:7), we shouldn't cast stones but should instead examine our own tendencies and track records. Even then, our self-orientation often blinds us to how unmerciful we can be. That's why it's always good practice to submit ourselves to the Lord's scrutiny in the humble spirit of the psalmist who prayed, "Search me, God, and know my heart; test me and know my anxious thoughts. See if there is any offensive way in me" (Ps. 139:23–24).

Here are some examples to show how we also might have rationalized unforgivingness had we been in the unmerciful servant's position. In each case, I will identify a possible root excuse and then share a few variations.

The "Difference" Excuse

The root excuse: I'm grateful my debt was forgiven, but his debt differs from mine, because …

- it was his fault he got into debt. I couldn't help my debt. It was due to a whole set of circumstances over which I had no control.

- he never pays people back. I realize my debt was larger, but he keeps borrowing money and not repaying other people, not just me. Someone needs to teach him a lesson.

Can you see yourself in either of these? We self-justify like this all the time. We tend to see our circumstances as unique. When we have problems, we are quick to understand why those problems happened in a way that casts us in a positive light, or at least we think, *There's nothing I could have done.* When other people have the same problems, we are quick to connect those problems to a flaw or failure on their part.

Let's not be so quick to cast stones. And remember, this parable does not explain the unmerciful servant's behavior, because there is no excuse. It doesn't matter why a person racks up a debt, even though some debts occur by unwise choices and others by uncontrollable circumstances. God's Old Testament provision for the "year for canceling debts" every seven years (Deut. 15:1) and the "year of jubilee" every fifty years (Lev. 25:10) mandates the cancellation of debts and restoration of lost property regardless of whether a person was to blame for being in debt or was simply a victim of unfortunate circumstances.

This spirit of "jubilee" applies not only to financial indebtedness. When people "owe" you more gratitude or thoughtfulness than they've shown or when they "owe" you an apology or a better attitude or kinder words, you have no more right to demand those "debts" be paid than the unmerciful servant had to demand payment. These offenses of sin and neglect are most likely what Jesus had in mind when He taught us to pray, "Forgive us our debts, as we also have forgiven our debtors" (Matt. 6:12).

When you hear yourself using the "difference" excuse to justify treating a person with a lack of grace and forgiveness, stop. Just stop. You have no excuse for using the "difference" excuse.

The "Obligation" Excuse

The root excuse: don't get me wrong; I am so relieved to have my debt canceled! But just because the master was obligated to cancel mine does not obligate me to cancel other people's debts. The master was obliged to cancel mine, because ...

- he's rich. He can afford to forgive my debt. He has plenty of money and won't go without food if he doesn't have my money. But the very fact that I couldn't pay the debt means I don't know whether I will even have enough money to put groceries on the table unless people who owe me pay me back. So the guy has got to pay up. A couple bucks is a couple bucks!

- there's a certain logic to debt repayment. If it's impossible to pay, then it might as well be erased. But when a debt is not too large to be repaid, then the obligation should be enforced. Consequently, the master was right not to enforce my debt, because it was unpayable. But I am justified in enforcing the debt of the guy who owes me, because it's payable.

A person who wants to find a law for everything makes these kinds of excuses. If there's obligation, then act. If there's no obligation, then there's no need to act. Again, this is a very common way we process moral decisions. Peter was coming from this perspective when he asked Jesus how many times he was expected to forgive someone. "Up to seven times?" (Matt. 18:21). How long am I obligated to forgive? Give me a black-and-white rule I can follow.

Jesus' answer—"seventy-seven times" (v. 22)—along with this elaborate parable reorients the question of forgiveness away from law toward grace. Unfortunately, most of us have not completed that reorientation, and we still function and justify ourselves according to whether we have fulfilled the laws of obligation rather than the law of love.

The "I'm Only Human" Excuse

The root excuse: I shouldn't have come down so strongly on that guy—maybe I even should have just let him off the hook—but I'm only human. You can't expect me …

- to act perfectly all the time. I was having a bad day and had a splitting headache. Plus, my stupid car just broke down again. So great … I had my debt forgiven, but I still didn't have enough money to get my car repaired. On another day, I probably would have been kinder in the way I approached the guy. But you need to understand I'm only human. It was the buildup of pressure.

- to be someone I'm not. I'm hotheaded. It's in my blood. It's just the way I am. Actually, that trait is usually a good thing; it's how I get things done. I'm aggressive in a good way. So when occasionally it works out in a negative way, cut me some slack, okay?

We do not give these excuses *before* we act poorly, but we use them to justify our behavior *after* the fact. We live in a culture that feeds us a steady diet of these kinds of excuses. We hear them on the news almost nightly. The CEO of a billion-dollar company gets caught on video using blistering epithets or racist language and defends himself by saying, "This is not who I really am. I'm not that kind of person." A group of teens take a video of a drowning man and do nothing to help and the parents defend their kids: "That's not who they are. They made a mistake."

Even in Christian circles, people excuse their wrong behavior or lack of love as a function of their personality type or their place in the birth order or their love language ("That's not my love language"). All these excuses boil down to this "I'm only human" idea with the implicit "You can't necessarily expect anything different and certainly can't fault me if I fall short of *your* expectations."

Yes, we each have a certain personality type that makes it easier or harder to behave in certain ways for the better or worse. And yes, birth order, upbringing, and social experiences all shape us. But there is no UOC version of the Bible that allows us to insert the phrase "*unless, of course*" after admonitions to love people, as in "Love your neighbor as yourself, *unless, of course*, you've had a frustrating day." Or "Bless those who mistreat you, *unless, of course*, you're at the end of your rope." Our God promises to conform us to His image as we by faith shed the "I'm only human" view of ourselves.

This famous parable that makes it so natural for us to join the onlookers and scorn the unmerciful servant should instead call us to look in the mirror, see our similarities to the unforgiving servant, and drop our stones. The spirit of forgiveness has no limit. No more excuses.

20/20 FOCUS

1. Compare the harsh words Jesus put in the mouth of the master toward the unmerciful servant with some other portion of Scripture that is similarly unforgiving toward unforgivingness.

2. This chapter focuses on our human tendency to rationalize attitudes of unforgivingness. What other things do human beings tend to rationalize? Make a list and identify the top two situations you rationalize.

3. We considered three "reasonable rationalizations" for the unmerciful servant's behavior. Can you think of any other? Here's a hint: think of someone you're having a hard time forgiving and listen to what you've been telling yourself.

Lord Jesus, this chapter has confronted me with my own tendency to rationalize unforgivingness. But Your Word also warns me about how difficult it is to know my own heart. Are there situations I've been rationalizing, especially in the area of unforgivingness, that I'm not even aware of? I'm

*nervous about what I might see, but I know I need
to. So search me and see if there is any offensive
way in me, and lead me onto Your path of mercy
and grace. Thank You. Amen.*

VISION CHECK

Storytellers often leave gaps—undescribed moments between
the actions when a character would have had to think or do
something that triggers the next recorded action. Since it is
not stated, you can't know for sure. But you can often make
reasonable assumptions about some things that might have
gone on.

Try stepping inside this major gap: the young disciple, John
Mark, who eventually wrote the gospel of Mark, once deserted
Paul on the world's first Christian mission trip. And Paul was so
upset he refused to give Mark a second chance. This created an
irreconcilable disagreement between Paul and Barnabas (read
Acts 15:37–40). As time went on, Paul must have had a change
of heart, because he later wrote approvingly about Mark (read
2 Tim. 4:11). Create a brief narrative to explain what might
have happened sometime between what Paul said in Acts 15
and what he wrote in 2 Timothy 4. Compare your imagined
scenario with mine on dougnewton.com or the Fresh Eyes app.

6

THESE WORDS? WHAT WORDS?

The Wise and Foolish Builders
Matthew 7:24–27

Jesus gave tons of commands. Having
a hard time obeying them all? One
tip leads to great optimism.

You've heard of mass communication theory? I have a *mis*communication theory: many cases of miscommunication can be traced back to the use of pronouns that lack clear antecedents, a topic I touched on earlier. I'll explain my theory in more depth in a moment, but I need to give you a more detailed review of pronouns and antecedents than I did in chapter 4. First, though, a refresher. A pronoun is a word that takes the place of a noun or noun phrase: *he, she,* or *it; they* or *them; this, that, those,* or *these; who, whom,* or *which*—just to name a few. Thus, every pronoun requires an antecedent, a previously mentioned noun to which it can refer.

The idea of the pronoun-antecedent relationship is simple. You can't use pronouns like *it* or *she* or *that* until you have identified what *it, she,* or *that* you are talking about. You can't just walk up to a friend or stranger and begin a conversation with "*It* may happen today if you're not careful," because the other person will wonder what *it* you're talking about. Or "If *she* starts coming your way, don't even stop." *She* who? Or "*That* is not something you should buy." What *that* are you talking about?

With that reminder, we can delve a bit more into pronouns. Some are called "demonstrative pronouns" because they not only have antecedents but also point to the location of that antecedent—they "demonstrate" whether the person or thing is nearby (e.g., *this* or *these*) or farther away (e.g., *that* or *those*). These demonstrative pronouns are particularly important in my miscommunication theory: many cases of miscommunication can be traced back to the use of pronouns that lack clear antecedents. I have tested *it* (notice the pronoun referring to the miscommunication theory?) for more than forty years of ministry and marriage, so I believe it is a sound theory. Plus, I maintain that if everyone paid more attention to the importance of this theory, much conflict in relationships could be prevented. Here's a common scenario: a wife arrived home from work and said to her husband, "I've been thinking a lot about the talk we had this morning before we left the house. I'm glad we did *that*."

So far so good. She used the pronoun *that*, clearly referring to the talk they had before going to work. "I'm glad too," he replied. But he quickly discovered she was pleased with the talk itself but not with what he actually said, because she continued, "But I can't believe you think *that*."

There's that *that* again, but this time it referred to something other than the talk per se. And here's where the conversation unnecessarily went off the rails. He assumed she was referring to his comment about her parents' overbearing tendencies and not wanting them to stay so long after Christmas. So he replied, "Why wouldn't I think *that*? Just look at the evidence. *It's* staring you right in the face."

He used two pronouns—*that* and *it*—referring to the way her parents meddle and make comments about how they don't keep their house in good order. But she wasn't talking about her parents when she said, "I can't believe you think *that*." She was talking about her weight-control struggle. What? Why did her mind go there? Because earlier that morning he mentioned the fact that they needed to get back to the gym as soon as the holidays were over as another reason her parents shouldn't stay long.

That comment held twice as much importance to her than he thought it did. She assumed he was commenting on her size. So after he said, "Why wouldn't I think *that*? Just look at the evidence," well, let's just say the peace of Christ was not present in their home for the rest of the week. Instantly the conversation escalated from *that* misunderstanding—which never got cleared up, by the way—to two hours of trading accusations that began with her saying, "You never support me; you're always so critical." And all because of their different interpretations of the pronoun *that*.

Pay attention to a miscommunication problem and see if demonstrative pronouns—*this*, *that*, *these*, and *those*—are contributing to the problem. Whenever you notice a demonstrative pronoun, be very careful to identify the antecedent!

Taking care with demonstrative pronouns not only avoids unnecessary conflict but also brings helpful clarity, as we will see in this chapter's focus on the parable of the wise and foolish builders. Remember how *that* goes?

> Therefore everyone who hears *these* words of mine and puts *them* into practice is like a wise man who built his house on the rock. The rain came down, the streams rose, and the winds blew and beat against *that* house; yet it did not fall, because it had its foundation on the rock. But everyone who hears *these* words of mine and does not put *them* into practice is like a foolish man who built his house on sand. The rain came down, the streams rose, and the winds blew and beat against *that* house, and it fell with a great crash. (Matt. 7:24–27)

This classic parable supports the biblical maxim found in James 1:22: "Be doers of the word, and not hearers only" (NKJV). Jesus promised that doers of the Word will be unshakable and resilient in the midst of life's storms. But foolish non-doers are sitting ducks subject to hurricane-like destruction. Any sensible person will want to prepare for the worst through diligently putting Jesus' words "into practice."

HUNTING FOR THE ANTECEDENT

Now we come to the all-important pronouns *these* and *them* when Jesus said, "Therefore everyone who hears *these* words of mine and puts *them* into practice …" What is the antecedent of *these* and *them*? If putting *them* into practice is so crucial—almost a life or death matter—then we need to know what words He had in mind.

Some people might say, "It doesn't matter whether you identify *exactly* which words He had in mind. Just gather up all Jesus' words wherever we find them and practice them *all*."

Granted, that's the safest thing to do. But ultimately it's not very helpful. If you're teaching your sixteen-year-old son to drive and you want to make sure he drives safely after he gets his license, sure, you could say, "Just remember *everything* I've taught you about driving and you'll come home in one piece every day." But if you really understand how dangerous it is to be out on the highways these days with fast cars, heavy traffic, text-distracted drivers, and some drivers who may even be under the influence of alcohol or drugs, then undoubtedly you want him to diligently follow certain key admonitions. Telling him to "just remember everything" lacks the kind of focus that will help keep his attention on the most important actions to ensure his safety. You will want him to practice particular "words of yours" like these:

- Do not text while you're driving.

- Do not play your music loud.

- Do not be goofing around with your friends.

- Watch out whenever you're approaching an intersection.

In the same way, while it may seem reasonable to practice everything Jesus said in the Gospels, that too lacks the kind of focus we need if we are to avoid the specific life-demolishing circumstances Jesus warned about. Plus, the placement of Jesus' parable as His concluding remarks in the Sermon on the Mount should restrict our search for the antecedent of *these words of mine* to within the sermon itself. That is what we will do in just a moment, as soon as we look at an important viewpoint on this most famous sermon.

HOW THE BIBLE IS GOD'S WORD

Many scholars debate whether the Sermon on the Mount is a sermon Jesus preached all at once or a collection of some of His famous sayings that were spoken at different times. Why is this important? If Matthew 5–7 is not one sermon preached all at once, then perhaps the antecedent to *these words of mine* can be found anywhere in the Gospels. If, however, this is a stand-alone sermon, then we should confine our search for the antecedent to Matthew 5–7. So which is it?

Matthew certainly presented it as one sermon, as I believe it is. However, even conservative New Testament scholars recognize how the gospel writers occasionally presented variations and rearrangements of Jesus' words and actions in order to make their theological points. What did He actually say and when? That's the question we often face as we study the biblical record. There were no recorders or cameras capturing Jesus' teaching moments. Are the words in red ink word-for-word quotations? Detailed paraphrases? Rough recollections of Jesus' teachings?

It's interesting to ask those questions. However, I don't believe we have to answer them in order to approach Scripture as God's Word with great confidence. Still, you may ask, "But if the Sermon on the Mount as Matthew recorded is not exactly what Jesus said word-for-word and if He did not speak it all at the same time in one sermon, then how can we have confidence in Scripture as God's Word?"

Consider this: What makes a portion of the Bible like the Sermon on the Mount a bona fide part of God's Word to human beings? Does it have to be an exact transcript of what Jesus said? Suppose I am talking to a friend and tell him some good things about my wife. Does my wife need a complete transcript from him of what I said? Or is it just as good if that friend says to my wife,

"You should hear what your husband thinks of you. He is in awe of your strength and grace and is sure there isn't a more wonderful person on earth!" Even though he isn't quoting me verbatim, he has delivered the intent and meaning of my words accurately.

In the same way, whether or not we have an exact transcript of Jesus' words, the Holy Spirit is that divine friend who delivers the intent and meaning of Jesus' words accurately. Perhaps He enabled the writers to remember Jesus' exact words. That's not hard for me to believe. Or perhaps the human authors used their memories to the best of their ability, but the Holy Spirit prompted and helped them organize their best recollections in such a way that not only preserved Jesus' teachings but also best served the church over the centuries.

In other words, I have what might be called a Trinitarian view of Scripture's creation. The Father is the *ideation*—the source of the Word. The Son is the *incarnation* who declared and demonstrated the Word by His physical presence—and still does. The Spirit is the *inspiration*, responsible for these processes:

- *recalling and transmitting* the words during the oral stage so they would be preserved accurately.

- *recording and translating* the words so they would be passed on faithfully in written form across the ages and among all people groups.

- *declaring and understanding* the words so they would be spoken with their original authority and received with penetrating power.

Together the three persons of the Trinity collaborated in harmony with one another. The Son spoke and lived the Father's words (John 12:49–50), and the Spirit both spoke Jesus' words (John 14:26) and inspired Jesus' followers as they wrote them (2 Tim. 3:16; 2 Pet. 1:20–21).

The symbiotic work of all three persons of the Trinity is what creates the Word of God and makes it authentic and authoritative, not just the isolated moment Jesus verbalized words to a group of people on a hillside. Because that comprehensive process involved all three persons of the Trinity working through human authors, transcribers, church councils, and translators, what we have before us today is what God wanted us to have. We should, therefore, relate to Scripture not as an enigmatic puzzle to be questioned but as an infallible document that does not fail to deliver eternal truth.

Therefore, because Matthew recorded a stream of Jesus' teaching as a sermon spoken all at once, that's how we should relate to it. That's how we will get the most out of it. And therefore, since it concludes with Jesus having said, "Everyone who hears *these* words of mine and puts *them* into practice," we should look for the antecedent to *these* and *them* within the body of that so-called sermon. I think that's the way the Holy Spirit wanted it to come to us. So let's do that now.

A STUDY IN CONTRASTS

A total of 2,346 words compose the Sermon on the Mount in the New International Version. When Jesus used the pronoun *these* in "these words of mine," was He referring to all 2,346? It appears not. We can narrow "these words" down considerably based on the fact that Jesus then said "and puts *them* into practice" ("does them" in the Greek). So we need look only for admonitions (i.e., things a person can do). But then we can narrow the list down even more by looking for admonitions related to contrasting behaviors or attitudes. Why should we do that?

Notice that this parable is a contrast parable: the wise man *versus* the foolish man. Often when Jesus used the contrast format in His parables, He was confronting the Pharisees and drawing a distinction between their values and those of His kingdom. A large portion of the Sermon on the Mount functions that way. It took Jesus only 343 words before He reached the part where He began to create this prophetic contrast: "For I tell you that unless your righteousness surpasses that of the Pharisees and the teachers of the law, you will certainly not enter the kingdom of heaven" (Matt. 5:20).

Just like the warning element directed toward the foolish builder in the parable, this verse warns those who think that the Pharisees' righteousness standard is satisfactory in God's eyes. Jesus then proceeded to contrast the ethical standards of His kingdom with the lower standards of the Pharisees. Therefore, the admonitions contained within this *framework of contrasts* constitute the most likely antecedents for *"these words mine"* that Jesus would have His hearers practice.

- Don't avoid just murder; avoid anger altogether (5:21–22).

- Don't presume to worship God until you have humbled yourself enough to make peace with your fellow believer (vv. 23–24).

- Don't avoid just adultery; avoid sexually illicit imaginations (vv. 27–30).

- Be so truthful you don't even need to swear an oath to be believed (vv. 33–37).

- When people mistreat you, do not seek retribution, even when it's just and your right to do so. Instead, bless and serve those people (vv. 38–47).

- Do not attempt to elevate yourself in other people's eyes by drawing attention to your good deeds (6:1–18).

A few other admonitions in the sermon also fall into this category of "surpassing righteousness," but these are enough to make the point.

IMPOSSIBLE COMMANDS, INCREDIBLE PROMISE

So far we have seen how the antecedent of "*these* words of mine" should be found within the confines of the Sermon on the Mount as recorded in Matthew 5–7. Specifically, the antecedent is the collection of admonitions Jesus gave concerning righteousness that surpasses that of the Pharisees. Let me explain the benefit of narrowing our search down to these few admonitions.

Simply put, you now have something much more specific to focus on as you answer the question: If I want to live my life on an unshakable foundation, to what should I pay careful attention? The answer: pay careful attention to Jesus' commands for surpassing righteousness.

Try reading those commands again. You may be overwhelmed. Avoid anger altogether? Never seek retribution?

You've got to be kidding! That standard for entering the kingdom of heaven seems virtually impossible. And it's a standard made seemingly more impossible by Jesus' summary admonition: "Be perfect, therefore, as your heavenly Father is perfect" (Matt. 5:48).

What is a person to do in the face of such an impossible standard? You have two options. One is to throw up your hands and fall on God's grace, trusting in what theologians call *imputed* righteousness. You confess your selfishness and sinful nature that render your own moral perfection impossible and rely solely on the righteousness of Jesus Christ, the only Perfect One, to cover you in the eyes of a holy God. As the old hymn says,

> My hope is built on nothing less
> Than Jesus' blood and righteousness.
> I dare not trust the sweetest frame,
> But wholly trust in Jesus' Name.
> On Christ the solid Rock I stand,
> All other ground is sinking sand.[1]

Trusting in His righteousness is "credited" to you as righteousness, which is fundamentally how *saving* grace works. But too often Christians stop there and slap bumper stickers on their cars that read, "I'm not perfect, just forgiven."

The other option in the face of the "impossible" standard of moral perfection is *not* to throw up your hands in resignation but to lean intently toward moral regeneration, to believe that God is calling you to a life of holy character. God's purpose and promise then is to *impart* His righteousness to you through the Holy Spirit's indwelling, recreating work. This goes beyond *saving* grace; He offers *sanctifying* grace.

Let's look at some facts revealed in this sermon. When Jesus told His disciples that their righteousness must surpass that of the Pharisees, His examples of countering anger, impurity, revenge, and self-promotion set a standard for our behavior here and now. If someone had asked Jesus, "Do You really mean we're supposed to be able to turn our other cheek and not get angry?" He would have said yes. These are *actual* expectations of *actual* behavior for *actual* people to exhibit *actual* righteousness. According to this parable, it's our practice of *these* words of Jesus, these admonitions of surpassing righteousness, that place us on solid ground instead of sinking sand.

Therein lies the great optimism behind the impossible standard. Every command of God contains an implied promise. Simply put, if God commands something, then obeying that command is possible. God, in His moral perfection, would never command a person to do what he or she cannot do.

The kind of righteousness we long for, the kind of relief from selfishness and sin we need, is available now. In heaven, there will be no temptations of anger, lust, revenge, or self-promotion. At that time these commands become unnecessary, so this kind of righteousness is both required and possible here and now. You can be the kind of person whose heart is fully inclined toward peace instead of anger, purity instead of impurity, grace instead of grievance, humility instead of hubris. That's great news!

Becoming this kind of person does not happen all at once. It's a gradual work over time. We are being made new (Rom. 12:1–2; Eph. 4:23) and changed incrementally (2 Cor. 3:18) as we choose to put off falsehood and put on truthfulness, to put off anger and put on gentleness, to speak only words that encourage and strengthen others (Eph. 4:25–32). Every choice is like opening a window to a fresh breeze of God's righteousness that fills us with power to "will and to act in order to fulfill his good purpose" (Phil. 2:13). In this process, we are actually fulfilling Paul's admonition—"Therefore, be imitators of God" (Eph. 5:1 ESV)—which echoes Jesus' call to "be perfect" in the Sermon on the Mount.

When you look at yourself and think about your struggles, it may be hard to see things this way. But that transformation process is what God wants and makes possible; it is what is going on as you cooperate and don't "grieve the Holy Spirit" (Eph. 4:30). God is faithful. "He who began a good work in you will carry it on to completion" (Phil. 1:6).

Let that optimism grip your heart as you consider this parable and its reference to such lofty words of Jesus. When you say and do everything with that optimism, that confidence in

God's promise and in His ability to make you truly righteous like Jesus is the rock you're standing on. Your hope is sure. What's more, as it turns out, you are becoming a demonstrative pronoun, pointing back to Jesus, our righteous antecedent.

20/20 FOCUS

1. Over the years, many scholars have questioned the reliability of quotations attributed to Jesus in the Gospels. While it is true there were no recorders or transcribers at the time, can you come up with at least three reasons we can trust the accuracy of quotations such as those found in the Sermon on the Mount?

2. Review the specific commands this chapter suggests Jesus was referring to when He said "these words of mine." Why would obedience to these commands in particular place a person on a firm foundation in life?

3. This chapter presents an optimistic view concerning *actual* human righteousness. It claims that every command of God implies a promise of what's possible, because God "would never

command a person to do what he or she cannot do." If you agree, can you name some commands other than those highlighted in this chapter that imply incredible possibilities for a human being?

Lord Jesus, I thank You that Your words bring life and hope. And most incredibly, the very words You tell me to obey bring the promise of obedience. I can't lose as long as I make Your words the standard for my life. So that's what I'm committing to right now—obedience to those impossible standards of righteousness with You as my hope and helper. Amen.

VISION CHECK

It is important to pay special attention to demonstrative pronouns. Whenever you see *this*, *that*, *these*, or *those* used in a sentence, always stop to make sure you know exactly what each pronoun is pointing to. Doing so improves your chances of seeing something new in the Scripture passage.

Here's an example to try. John told of a well-known moment when Jesus asked Peter three times, "Do you love me?" The first time, Jesus asked, "Do you love me more than *these*?"

(John 21:15). To what was Jesus referring when He used the demonstrative pronoun *these*? If you figure that out, you might see this special moment in a different way than it is often portrayed. (Hint: read Matt. 26:31–35.) Check out my insights on dougnewton.com or the Fresh Eyes app and compare them with yours.

7

AN OVERDONE AND UNDERDONE "WELL DONE"

The Five Talents
Matthew 25:14–30

Wouldn't it be nice if you could hear
God say "Well done" before you die?

I've been part of so many funerals during my pastoral ministry I think I should be excused from my own. Because I've participated in so many, I can easily tell you the top five most commonly heard expressions at funerals. Coming in at number 5: "Doesn't he (or she) look so peaceful?" For your information, this also happens to be number one on the list of the top five lies told at funerals.

Number 4: "If I never hear another bagpipe rendition of 'Amazing Grace,' it'll be too soon." Number 3: "She is singing with the angels today." And rounding out the top five is a two-way tie for first place:

- "Well done, good and faithful servant."

- "I never heard him (or her) say a cross word to anyone."

If you need me to break the tie between these two finalists, the award goes to the "Well done" statement—and not only because it comes directly from the Bible. The one about never hearing a cross word should be disqualified on the grounds that it simply isn't believable. Not that people are lying. In the grief of the moment, I have no doubt tears of sorrow fog the memory and the misty light of sentimentality shines only on the dearly departed one's finest moments.

However, if it were true the deceased person never said a cross word, and given the fact that I have heard it said of 99 percent of the people lying in repose, one must wonder why the world isn't a kinder place. That remaining 1 percent of crabby people (whose funerals I have never performed) must get around as miraculously as Santa on Christmas Eve, because the sound of cross words is as ubiquitous as blasting car horns in New York City during rush hour.

So "Well done, good and faithful servant" gets my vote as the number-one expression heard at funerals. Too bad it's a misunderstanding of the parable in which it is found.

I can sense your hackles rising, especially if you've said or heard this said about a departed loved one, so I should jump quickly to explain. The parable of the talents is found in a series of teachings and parables Jesus gave in response to the disciples requesting a timetable for the temple's destruction, which He had just predicted and which they assumed would signal the "end of the age" (Matt. 24:3). "Jesus left the temple and was walking away when his disciples came up to him to call his attention to its buildings. 'Do you see all these things?' he asked. 'Truly I tell you, not one stone here will be left on another; every one will be thrown down.' As Jesus was sitting on the Mount of Olives, the disciples came to him privately. 'Tell us,' they said, 'when will this happen, and what will be the sign of your coming and of the end of the age?'" (vv. 1–3).

In response Jesus gave many prophecies about world events and the disciples' upcoming persecution. What He said was couched in such apocalyptic language that many Christian teachers over the centuries have viewed Matthew 24–25 as a description of the so-called end times. Although there are many differences of opinion about the end times, the central dramatic event involves the second coming of Jesus. So scholars typically interpret Jesus' parables in this extended teaching section against that backdrop. Whether or not that should be the case remains an open question.

Regardless of how the end times will play out and when they began or will begin, Jesus used three parables and one dramatic scene to emphasize the importance of being ready at all times to account for one's faithfulness to the Lord. This parable of the talents is centrally located in that context. That's why Jesus began with the word *again*.

> Again, it will be like a man going on a journey, who called his servants and entrusted his wealth to them. To one he gave five bags of gold, to another two bags, and to another one bag, each according to his ability. Then he went on his

journey. The man who had received five bags of gold went at once and put his money to work and gained five bags more. So also, the one with two bags of gold gained two more. But the man who had received one bag went off, dug a hole in the ground and hid his master's money. (Matt. 25:14–18)

Then Jesus brought His listeners to that sobering moment of accountability when each of the three servants presented to the returning master the results of his efforts to steward the master's property.

After a long time the master of those servants returned and settled accounts with them. The man who had received five bags of gold brought the other five. "Master," he said, "you entrusted me with five bags of gold. See, I have gained five more."

His master replied, "Well done, good and faithful servant! You have been faithful with a few things; I will put you in charge of many things. Come and share your master's happiness!"

The man with two bags of gold also came. "Master," he said, "you entrusted me with two bags of gold; see, I have gained two more."

His master replied, "Well done, good and faithful servant! You have been faithful with a few things; I will put you in charge of many things. Come and share your master's happiness!" (vv. 19–23)

Let's pause in the flow of the story here, because the third servant's report resulted in condemnation, not the "Well done" commendation. That will take us to another matter we'll consider in a moment. So before we dig into that, let's deal with what I consider a misunderstanding that leads to the "Well done" expression being overused at funeral services.

PRE- OR POSTHUMOUS

Here's the issue: because this teaching section in Matthew 24–25 is fraught with end times language and images, regardless of how they are understood, it has become impossible, apparently, for people to imagine this moment of accountability, commendation, and reward from the master as anything but a final scene in heaven. In other words, we conceive of no other occasion when a person will hear these words from the Lord than after his or her life on earth is over. Hence, it is the number-one thing said at funerals. And yes, it is appropriate to say it then, but not exclusively then.

This accountability moment that promises the hope of commendation and reward is *not* necessarily awarded posthumously—that is, after the soul leaves the body to meet the Lord. Why should we think that? According to the master's own words, the moment of commendation and reward occurred *before* the servants completed their service for the master. Note that the master clearly indicated more work on his behalf remained to be done: "His master replied, 'Well done, good and faithful servant! You have been faithful with a few things; I will put you in charge of many things. Come and share your master's happiness!'" (Matt. 25:21).

Rather than the commendation-and-reward moment occurring at the end of a person's life, it appears to be midstream—*prehumous,* if that is a word. This aligns with what Jesus had already said to His disciples about faithful servanthood when He led up to the parables told in Matthew 25: "Who then is the faithful and wise servant, whom the master has put in charge of the servants in his household to give them their food at the proper time? It will be good for that servant whose master finds him doing so when he returns. Truly I tell you, he will put him in charge of all his possessions" (24:45–47).

It also concurs with the other version of this parable recorded in Luke's gospel, in which some significant differences appear. Yet both imply that the commendation-and-reward moment occurred when there was still work to be done. Luke's version ends by saying, "'Well done, my good servant!' his master replied. 'Because you have been trustworthy in a very small matter, take charge of ten cities'" (Luke 19:17).

While we all certainly hope to hear "Well done" at our deaths, it does not appear that the commendation-and-reward moment occurs only when our work on earth is done. Why is this important?

THE FATHER'S REASSURANCE

Think of how we imagine hearing these words of our Lord. That wonderful moment will bring relief and peace and will be a time when you can finally rest from your labors and enjoy the blissful experience of completion. Can it be we don't have to wait until we die to experience the sweet taste of that reward? What if we can enjoy that experience even in this life? Jesus seems to have confirmed that possibility when He promised "rest for your souls" to weary people if they work faithfully alongside Him in this life: "Come to me, all you who are weary and burdened, and I will give you rest. Take my yoke upon you and learn from me, for I am gentle and humble in heart, and you will find rest for your souls" (Matt. 11:28–29).

We don't have to wait until we go to our "eternal rest" to experience a soul-resting commendation and reward from the Lord as His response to our faithful service. And just think:

that means we can enter into His happiness in this life over who we are (though we are still in process) and what we have done (though we wish we could have done better)!

As a pastor, I have sat across the table from far too many people who choke back tears while describing their troubled relationship with a mother or father. I've seen grown men hang their heads and slump their shoulders in utter defeat as they say, "My dad never said 'I love you' or told me he was proud of me." Even as adults they longed for some assurance that their fathers loved and prized them.

I understand how important that is. My dad rarely gushed emotional words of love. Although I was a sports star on my high school and college teams, he rarely attended my games. He couldn't. People back then didn't have as much freedom to break away from work to sit on the sidelines and watch their kids play sports. My parents didn't applaud every breath I took or plaster every latest creation of mine on the fridge as if I was Andrew Wyeth. In fact, my dad was a stickler for excellence and didn't applaud anything that was not worthy of acclaim just to make someone feel good. But I never felt I had to measure up to some standard in order to be acceptable to him. Why?

Fortunately, there were times—moments of commendation and reward—that fed my sense of worth and grounded me in the unshakable assurance of his love. Like the day he dropped me off for my freshman year at college. The car was unloaded. Packed boxes crowded my dorm room. My mind had already focused on the all-important question of where to hang posters of Jimi Hendrix and Pelé. So Dad and I said good-bye, and he left to travel the two hours back home. About fifteen minutes later, a knock sounded on the door. It was Dad.

"What are you doing back?"

He was a little awkward when he said, "I just had to come back, because I wanted to look you in the eye when I said I love you. I'm proud of you, boy." Then he left again.

That was one of the most important moments of my life. I know what it feels like to have a father not just rattle off a few words of love but say them and mean them so deeply he had to turn around and drive an extra thirty miles just to tell me. That kind of affirmation and commendation can't be shaken. You don't have to hear it very often, because the stabilizing soul-rest it creates in a son lasts and lasts. According to this parable, we can experience that from our heavenly Father even before we die.

RISK AND REWARD

If this "Well done, good and faithful servant" experience is truly a possibility in this life, then we should be careful to understand who Jesus considers a faithful servant. Unfortunately, teachers often use this parable as a "perfect" lesson on stewardship. The moral of the story, we are told, is to use wisely and productively the resources the Lord has placed in our hands. Of course, that should be our desire, but that is not the story's moral. The key message is the part of the parable that is underdone.

Is the point really to be productive? No, the point is to *try* something, *anything* that will benefit the master to some degree. The first and second servants were not equally productive, yet they received the same commendation and reward. The master was angry with the third servant for letting fear render him fruitless. He was unwilling to take any risk with what he had been given. It turns out this parable is not so much about stewardship and productivity as it is about taking risks for the master's benefit. That is what pleases the Lord.

Remember, we are talking about the One who risked His reputation to associate with sinners (Matt. 9:10–11). The One who faced the charge of lawbreaker for healing on the Sabbath (12:9–13). The One who faced charges of blasphemy, because He not only healed a paraplegic man but also provided relief from the paralysis of sin (9:1–7). Obviously, He is not going to be pleased with someone who fears what he might lose if he tries to do something worthwhile for God. After all, He is the one who specifically denounced self-protection and promoted self-sacrifice: "For whoever wants to save their life will lose it, but whoever loses their life for me will find it" (16:25).

This parable's point is not that commendable stewardship equals success and productivity. No, the point is to honor the master's resources enough to make the master's business goals your priority; try something—anything—to be productive for him. My guess is that if any of the servants had come back and said, "I did my best to make something out of the money you gave me, but things did not work out as I hoped," the master would *not* have gotten angry at him. In other words, faithfulness means risk more than results.

In a world that places so much emphasis on success and productivity, average Christians like us can easily get the idea that good results equal success and poor results equal failure. That's why we hear only the success stories. However, here's the good news: in God's kingdom, faithfully risking all you've been given for His purposes and glory, regardless of the results, pleases the Lord and gives you the experience of "Well done" well before your casket closes.

20/20 FOCUS

1. Even though the point of this chapter is that we don't have to wait until our deaths to enjoy a sense of "Well done," it's still nice to think of that happening when we meet the Lord. Name a couple people you know who should get a resounding "Well done" at the end of their lives. Why? (How about writing them a note?)

2. What might Jesus have had in mind when He had the master say to the faithful servants, "I will put you in charge of many things"?

3. Think of something you have been doing recently that leaves you wondering whether the Lord is pleased with your efforts: *Am I doing this well enough? Am I accomplishing anything worthwhile?* (If you're sharing in a group right now, be vulnerable. It will help.)

4. Think of a time when you tried hard to do something good and right but failed. Based on the perspective presented in this chapter, can you hear what the Lord might be saying to you?

Lord Jesus, I know You don't require success in order to gain Your approval, but I often struggle with those kinds of thoughts. They bind me up and make me afraid. I second-guess myself all the time. Please give me a fresh revelation of Your grace toward me even when—especially when—I fail. Help me find relief in knowing that You are pleased with me as long as I am attempting to use Your resources in my life for Your glory and purposes. Amen.

VISION CHECK

Life is full of clichés. The trick is spotting them before they lead you into lazy agreement. They are not always wrong, but they should always be questioned.

Here's a famous Bible saying that is an ideal candidate for examination: "Perfect love casts out fear" (1 John 4:18 NKJV). Read the preceding context (chs. 3–4) to identify the specific problem John was addressing and see if we should adjust the way we use that cliché. You'll find my thoughts to compare with yours on dougnewton.com or the Fresh Eyes app.

8

THE TAMING OF THE SHREWD

The Shrewd Manager

Luke 16:1–9

How can such a confusing parable turn
out to offer such clear good news?

You've probably heard the popular adage, "It's not the destination; it's the journey." There's a lot of truth in it. We should learn to enjoy the processes of life, the day-to-day comings and goings. Don't just live head down, nose to the grindstone, pressing on toward lofty goals. Stop and smell the roses. Breathe deeply. Enjoy your fellow travelers. We miss too many of life's joys and blessings when we are so purpose-driven, goal-oriented, and seminar-motivated.

However, this "enjoy the journey" can also be nothing more than a sequel to the ancient motto, "Eat, drink, and be merry, for tomorrow we die." Embedded in this call to "smell the roses" is a long-recognized fatalism that does not square with truth. Ultimately, the destination validates the journey and brings the only lasting meaning to the things we attempt to enjoy.

As I write this chapter, one of my daughters has just delivered her third child. Believe me, for her it definitely was *not* the journey; it was the destination: *Get me to the hospital! There is one place and one place only I want to be, and I want to be there now!* What is it that helped her through the nauseating first trimester; the enormous discomforts of the third trimester; and the sharp, unrelenting contractions of a thirty-six-hour delivery? The promise of a destination that's worth it all. Holding a new gift from God in her arms.

For most people, life's journey consists of pleasant seasons to be enjoyed and dark days to be endured. The ratio of sunny to stormy days varies from person to person and even nation to nation. Certainly, wealthy nations have luxuries that make the hard times more bearable and often more avoidable. But all people go through extended hard times. And many people learn how to savor the smallest blessings and detect the slightest waft of a pleasant fragrance even amid the acrid atmosphere of war, destruction, drought, poverty, disease, and hunger. What makes that possible is a sustaining sense of something worth living for. A purpose. A distant landmark of promise, a horizon of hope for tomorrow.

My mom was eighty-six when she died. She lived in our home her final ten years. During her last four years, she dealt with (in chronological order) a separated shoulder that required months of therapy, the removal of her left lung at the same time my dad was dying, colon cancer and surgery, a heart attack, a stroke that robbed her of speech for the last three years of her life, and a broken hip necessitating more therapy.

George MacDonald referred to the body in old age as "undressing for its last sweet bed."[1] But my mom's plight was not just a matter of those creeping losses. She never did "rage against the dying of the light" as Dylan Thomas poetically urged.[2] Her later days were a complete muzzling of all forms of communication. Imagine getting to the place where you can't even make your right hand sign "Love, Mom" on your children's Christmas cards. She heroically tried to enjoy the journey, but ultimately not much was left in her but the longing for release and repose at her final destination. For many old folks, waking up and facing a new day is harder than anything I have yet to do in life. The only things that keep them going are the destination and some perfectly timed sensations of the nearness of Jesus.

So join me in taking a somewhat countercultural position in affirming the ultimate importance of *the destination*. That perspective seems to fit a major theme of Scripture reiterated in numerous ways, as we are told to

- set our heart and minds on things above (Col. 3:1–2).

- be like the heroes of our faith, who pursued a kingdom beyond this earth (Heb. 11:13–16).

- be like Jesus, who endured the cross because of the joy set before Him (Heb. 12:2).

- endure suffering patiently, knowing that we are achieving a far greater weight of glory (2 Cor. 4:17).

- endure persecution, knowing that a crown of life awaits (Rev. 2:10).

If you happen to currently enjoy the privilege of a comfortable life on earth, one full of opportunities for travel, discovery, and pleasures of your choosing (i.e., a satisfying journey), do not be lured into the cultural trap of neglecting the future. Press on toward the prize of the high calling we have in Christ. Jesus—knowing Him, loving Him, serving Him, and joining Him—is your destination. Count everything else as garbage in comparison (Phil. 3:8–14).

Why am I getting preachy about this? There's no way to make sense of the confusing parable we're about to discuss without turning your mind from an "enjoy the journey" mentality and shifting toward a destination mentality. It's a parable driven entirely by concern for future well-being and how to achieve it.

WHERE THE CONFUSION SNEAKS IN

As I said, this is a very confusing parable, because it seems to applaud the self-serving behavior of a person who sought to achieve a desired result through shady—or what is too graciously called "shrewd"—methods. Here's what he did.

As the manager of a rich man's possessions, he had been irresponsible and wasteful enough to get called into the corner office and be given a two-week termination notice. Now he had to think fast and develop a fallback plan before his final day at work, because he was a lazy bum too soft for hard work and too proud for panhandling (Luke 16:3).

Apparently, he had enough time to contact a few clients and discount their bills substantially enough to believe it might create a network of friends who would help him weather the storm until he found another job he could slither into. Here's how Jesus described his shrewd scheme:

> "I know what I'll do so that, when I lose my job here, people will welcome me into their houses."
>
> So he called in each one of his master's debtors. He asked the first, "How much do you owe my master?"
>
> "Nine hundred gallons of olive oil," he replied.
>
> The manager told him, "Take your bill, sit down quickly, and make it four hundred and fifty."
>
> Then he asked the second, "And how much do you owe?"

"A thousand bushels of wheat," he replied.

He told him, "Take your bill and make it
eight hundred." (vv. 4–7)

In the next verse, Jesus used a word that sparks much confusion. He said, "The master *commended* the dishonest manager because he had acted shrewdly" (v. 8).

The word *commended* makes us cock our heads as we struggle with what seems to be an approved behavior. The rich master valued and surprisingly approved the shrewd strategy of this admittedly dishonest manager. But even more shockingly, on the surface Jesus seemed to have joined that commendation by acknowledging that "people of this world" do a better job of being "shrewd" than God's people (v. 8). The Greek word translated "shrewd" in this verse usually has a very positive connotation—doing something beneficial—and is ordinarily translated "wise." Then Jesus went so far as to urge people to use monetary leverage to make friends for an ulterior purpose like the dishonest manager (v. 9).

Jesus seemed to have been saying that just as the dishonest manager connived a way to use money to make friends and secure his future welcome, we should do something similar to gain "friends" and ensure our welcome into an eternal home. Why does Jesus seem to have applauded such scheming?

Hoping to clear up the confusion, some commentators provide very helpful information about first-century business practices and the meaning of "friends" in this culture of hospitality. That is important information. But I want us to try to solve the puzzle by simply sticking to the text.

CONTRAST NOT COMPARISON

Unlike many of Jesus' parables, this one flows seamlessly from the story of the parable (Luke 16:1–8) to Jesus' commentary on it (vv. 9–13). It's hard to know—and, apparently, it's not important for us to know—where one ends and the other begins. Jesus seemingly didn't want us to draw a sharp line. Consequently, His commentary can help us understand the story's point. When we do that, we discover Jesus was not making a comparison at all. Instead, He was making a stark contrast.

- He talked about gaining welcome into people's earthly homes versus welcome into eternal dwellings (vv. 4, 9).

- He contrasted the shrewdness of worldly people with the lack of shrewdness of God's people (v. 8).

- He distinguished between trustworthiness and dishonesty (vv. 10–12).

- He concluded with a very strong contrast between serving God and serving money (v. 13). I say "a very strong contrast" because scholars tell us that in this culture it was common for slaves to serve two masters who had a cooperative agreement. So when Jesus said, "You *cannot* serve both God and money," He was claiming that it is impossible. There can be no cooperative agreement whatsoever between these two masters.

Jesus emphasized all these points of contrast when He turned to the listening and sneering Pharisees (v. 14), looked them in the eyes, and made a final, most telling contrast, one that helps us understand the parable: "What people value highly is detestable in God's sight" (v. 15).

That one comment clarifies the parable, for it tells us *not* to see the rich master's commendation as a good thing. Yes, the master valued and commended the dishonest manager's actions. But now we know, because Jesus spoke plainly about the stark contrast, that the rich man commended something that God detests. Ah, good to know. Now we can return to the parable and work through it, reassured that we are not supposed to admire or emulate the shrewd manager.

TAKE GOD OUT OF IT

Based on what we just discovered, we now realize that the rich master in the story *does not* represent God. Because so many parables position a master, king, or father as a God figure, it becomes habitual to assume that the authoritative figure in any parable represents God. This is not always the case, and it is definitely *not* the case in this parable.

In this parable, nothing about the rich man gives insight into God's nature, values, or behavior. Because of what we have already seen, we know that both the dishonest manager and the rich man are part of and functioning within an ungodly value system.

THE USE OF POSSESSIONS

As we have already seen, this parable must be read as a study in contrasts. Since it kicks off with a focus on accountability for the use of the rich man's possessions, we should concentrate on that as the fundamental contrast Jesus sought to illustrate. The shrewd manager's use and misuse of his master's possessions were detailed and clear: he was wasteful, corrupt, self-serving, and self-protecting. With whom is he being contrasted? The contrasting party is only implied. Jesus was calling His disciples to function differently, as bona fide "people of the light" (Luke 16:8). They were to use their heavenly Master's possessions in a way exactly opposite of what the shrewd manager did. If they lived by a contrasting set of values, they were promised eternal well-being, though not necessarily immediate well-being (v. 9).

So what way is the exact opposite of how the shrewd manager used the rich man's funds? The opposite of wasteful, corrupt, self-serving, and self-protecting. What kind of practical use does that imply? Here we must bring in the larger context of Jesus' teaching about the use of money and possessions. When we do that, there is no doubt He was talking about serving the poor, those who can do nothing for us and who cannot make it without us. All the gospel writers made this clear, but Luke elevated that theme through some of Jesus' quotations that he uniquely selected for his gospel.

- "The Spirit of the Lord is on me, because he has anointed me to proclaim good news to the poor. He has sent me to proclaim freedom for the prisoners and recovery of sight for the blind, to set the oppressed free, to proclaim the year of the Lord's favor" (4:18–19).

- "But seek his kingdom, and these things will be given to you as well. Do not be afraid, little flock, for your Father has been pleased

to give you the kingdom. Sell your possessions and give to the poor" (12:31–33).

- "When you give a luncheon or dinner, do
  not invite your friends, your brothers or sis-
  ters, your relatives, or your rich neighbors; if
  you do, they may invite you back and so you
  will be repaid. But when you give a banquet,
  invite the poor, the crippled, the lame, the
  blind, and you will be blessed. Although they
  cannot repay you, you will be repaid at the
  resurrection of the righteous" (14:12–14).

Then Luke continued emphasizing poverty relief in the book
of Acts when he called special attention to the early Christians'
Spirit-created concern for the poor.

All the believers were one in heart and mind.
No one claimed that any of their possessions
was their own, but they shared everything they
had.... There were no needy persons among
them. For from time to time those who owned
land or houses sold them, brought the money
from the sales and put it at the apostles' feet,
and it was distributed to anyone who had need.
(4:32–35)

These and many other allusions to poverty relief in Luke-Acts create an unmistakable context for understanding what Jesus considered the faithful use of worldly wealth in this parable.

If you are like me, this emphasis on rescuing the poor is not anything new, but my commitment to kingdom values like that constantly needs renewal. I tend to drift away from them. Everything we have been given belongs to God, not us, and is to be used in ways that fulfill our Master's desires. The Lord wants us to be as "shrewd" as the dishonest manager. But that shrewdness with its animal instinct for selfish gain must be tamed by a compassionate heart for those who God prioritizes: those who are poor in some way. This is a challenge, yet in that very fact we also find incredibly good news.

DIVINE POVERTY RELIEF

In my prayerful preparation for writing this chapter, one morning I found myself disappointed in myself for a variety of reasons. A month earlier I had suffered a severe bicycling accident that resulted in eight rib fractures, a life flight to a trauma center, and a long recovery time. Consequently, I was less focused and productive than I wanted to be about meeting some of my deadlines. I felt like I lost steam and concentration.

To top it off, I knew I had allowed the deadlines to rob me of devotional times with the Lord.

Then in my prayer time that morning—the first one I'd had in more than a week—as I sheepishly approached the Lord, asking for His help with this parable, I sensed Him saying, *I don't expect anything of the "people of the light" that I am not doing Myself. After all, I am the light. I am all about giving everything I have to those who are poor. If I am expecting you to regard the poor with generosity, wouldn't I be regarding you in the same way? When you are poor in effort, when you are poor in strength, when you are poor in wisdom or diligence or conviction, don't come to Me in shame. Come to Me in confidence and faith. I already am the kind of person I want you to be. So when you are poor in spirit, guess what? That's exactly when I plan to give you the kingdom of heaven. There's a reason I made that My very first beatitude.*

Perhaps this parable leaves you overwhelmed with the standard of self-sacrifice Jesus set, unsure about the cost, but certain about having fallen short. If this challenging parable ultimately presents us with the Master's demand, then it also reveals His nature. When you lack the necessary compassion, He will provide you with the resources of heart and mind necessary to handle His wealth—material or spiritual—in ways that please Him. Consequently, in this life we get to sample the riches of God's eternal kingdom, our eternal home into which we will one day be welcomed. This one truth makes the journey almost as grand as the destination.

20/20 FOCUS

1. If you're like most people, something strikes you as wrong about the behavior of the shrewd manager, even though the rich man commended him. Don't just "feel" that way; try to put it into words. Things often become clearer when you hunt for the right words.

2. Why do you think the master commended the dishonest manager? What impressed him? What did Jesus want us to be impressed by?

3. Ultimately, hearing Jesus call the worldly values and resulting behavior of the shrewd manager "detestable in God's sight" brings us relief. What do you think falls into that category of detestable values?

4. For a refresher in what God highly values, read aloud Jeremiah 5:23–29; 22:3–5. Where might

your values need to align more closely with the Lord's?

Lord Jesus, this was a hard chapter for me to read. I am prone to neglect the poor—to see them as victims of their own poor choices; to absolve myself of responsibility based on my own needs for money, shelter, and safety; and to take wise steps to secure my own future as my priority. This parable calls me to a different value system. I'm going to need the Holy Spirit's help to live out those values, especially since I'm often unaware of the times I'm caught up in the world's values. Please help. Amen.

VISION CHECK

Our instincts are notoriously untrustworthy, especially when compared with the trustworthiness of God's Word. Yet sometimes your gut makes you wonder whether the widely held understanding of some portion of God's Word is correct. In those times, it is appropriate to question—humbly!—whether the common point of view is correct.

Here's a controversial contemporary issue to consider. Read Paul's statement in 1 Corinthians 14:34 about women keeping silent in church. How does your gut react to that? The point is not to force your opinion to change but to let your mind follow your gut long enough to rethink the issue in relation to the whole counsel of God. Maybe something new will come to mind. Maybe not. At least you're giving the Lord a chance to help you see something with fresh eyes. Feel free to compare your thoughts with mine on dougnewton.com or the Fresh Eyes app.

9

WHAT "ONE" ARE WE TALKING ABOUT?

The Lost Sheep

Luke 15:1–7; Matthew 18:10–14

How far can you stretch a parable?

Here's something you'll never hear: "Take Me Out to the Ball Game" sung as the bride walks down the aisle. Or "Pomp and Circumstance" at a funeral. Or "Hail to the Chief" at the grand opening of a neighborhood fast-food restaurant. Context is everything in determining what is appropriate.

On our wedding day, just minutes before my bride's father was to escort her down the aisle—the prelude music was already playing, and I was about to step onto the platform with the officiating pastor—my jokester soon-to-be father-in-law greeted his daughter, wearing crusty farm boots, bib overalls, a flannel shirt, a crumpled cowboy hat, and a huge smile on his face. I had no idea what was going on out in the church lobby, but my wife-to-be was mortified! After a good laugh, her dad quickly changed and the wedding proceeded with the one desired "hitch." Context is everything. Weddings call for tuxedos and cummerbunds, not yee-haws and bandanas.

However, most music, dress, and activities are like elastic. They fit many contexts just fine. On that same wedding day, our "very Christian" ceremony featured music from Motown and Mendelssohn. Both were appropriate—just not as the bridal processional. Nevertheless, it's always important to ask, "Is this appropriate?" or you may wind up coming as a Tootsie Roll to an Overeaters-Anonymous Halloween party.

Many of Jesus' parables are also elastic. Even though they have a specific context in Scripture, they also can be properly applied in various settings. The parable of the lost sheep provides a case in point. Matthew and Luke recorded very similar versions of this parable, but each chose to refer to it for a different reason. In other words, this parable "stretched" to fit more than one context. I want to demonstrate how that works in this chapter and why it is important to take advantage of its elasticity.

ELASTIC THREADS

Let's first review how similar the versions are. The story line is essentially the same with only slight but interesting variations. So I have interlaced them. Luke's version is in roman type and Matthew's is in italics.

> *What do you think?* Suppose one of you has (*If a man owns*) a hundred sheep and loses one of them (*and one of them wanders away*). Doesn't he leave the ninety-nine in the open country (*on the hills*) and go after (*go to look for*) the

lost sheep (*the one that wandered off*) until he finds it? And when he finds it (*if he finds it*), he joyfully puts it on his shoulders and goes home. Then he calls his friends and neighbors together and says, "Rejoice with me; I have found my lost sheep." (*truly I tell you, he is happier about that one sheep than about the ninety-nine that did not wander off*)

You can see the story in both is the same. A person is missing just one of his one hundred sheep, but he leaves the ninety-nine to search for it. He finds the sheep and rejoices. Matthew's version differs only by explaining how the sheep got lost ("wanders off") and leaving out the element of community celebration ("calls his friends and neighbors together …") mentioned by Luke.

However, the two versions differ significantly in another important way. Matthew and Luke referred to this parable for different reasons. That's why I talk about this parable as having elasticity. Matthew introduced the parable after Jesus focused attention on the nature of children and their need for protection. Immediately after the disciples questioned Jesus about the kingdom of heaven's ranking system—"Who, then, is the greatest?" (Matt. 18:1)—He invited a child to stand with Him as an object lesson for several points He made in response (vv. 2–10):

- "Unless you change and become like little children, you will never enter the kingdom of heaven."

- "Whoever welcomes one such child in my name welcomes me."

- "If anyone causes one of these little ones— those who believe in me—to stumble, it would be better for them to have a large millstone hung around their neck and to be drowned in the depths of the sea."

- "See that you do not despise one of these little ones. For I tell you that their angels in heaven always see the face of my Father in heaven."

While these comments seem random on the surface, they are tied together by the way they flip upside down the common attitude toward children, who often went unnoticed, unprotected, and unrespected in Jesus' day.

In contrast, Luke included this parable as part of Jesus' reaction when the Pharisees muttered about Him sharing meals with tax collectors and "sinners" (Luke 15:1–2). It was the first of three parables (lost sheep, lost coin, lost son), which all illustrate heaven's joy-filled response when lost people are found and repent (see chapter 3 of this book). Jesus implied His sharing meals with scorned sinners—a very important element of building relationships in this culture—was part of seeking and finding the lost.

FORSAKING FOR SEEKING

Here again, looking only at the surface, the contexts for the two versions of the parable are markedly distinct. One refers to honoring and protecting children. The other defends the evangelistic value of associating with common sinners. However, just as a single elastic band can stretch to fit various objects, as Matthew and Luke demonstrated, Jesus' parable also stretches to fit various circumstances. Nevertheless, we can still identify a shared theme. What is that theme? Go to great lengths to protect or rescue persons who tend to go unnoticed.

But that's not all. Jesus also valued going to great lengths on behalf of *the lost one* even if it means leaving behind *the sheltered ninety-nine*. But a shepherd is responsible for the whole flock! To leave them alone for the sake of just one lost sheep would have seemed risky. That act of turning away from them would have felt negligent and uncaring. Nevertheless, Jesus' emphasis on *the lost one* implies this.

On my very first Sunday as the pastor of a renowned college church in my denomination, I entered the pulpit to preach without a suit and tie and continued to do so the remainder of my eleven years there. In many churches around our country this would have been no problem. But in this rather traditional setting, many of the longtime members did not appreciate this. I "heard" about it occasionally. Even though I always came clean and pressed, I knew my lack of decorum for a Sunday service disturbed some people. However, this "lost sheep" parable stretched to fit this situation, so their approval and Sabbath equilibrium could not be my concern. Of course, I did not want to cause offense, but they were among the ninety-nine. They were well cared for. Their lives were stable and relatively healthy. My concern was for the scores of people to whom the doors of our church were culturally closed because of its reputation as a highbrow congregation. My preaching in semi-casual dress, along with other gradual adjustments in the "air" of our environment, sent a message that we were a congregation of common people who wanted no one to feel out of place or not good enough to attend.

While this is trivial when compared with horrific injustices on a global scale, it is one example of how Jesus' elastic parable of the lost sheep can stretch over thousands of situations. In order to focus rescuing attention on one person or group, you will often have to forsake a large group of others who are already within the "fold" of care and privilege. Let me go even further. The lost sheep parable, along with its important elasticity, illustrates as well as any portion of Scripture the nature of our prime directive as Christians. Simply put, our mission is to find the one nobody notices, serves, or offers rescuing hope to.

FROM TEDDY TO TORNADOES

Of course, we can think of noticing and rescuing people—seeking *the one*—in terms of spiritual salvation. Where do we go to provide gospel ministry to those who have never heard? That's how this parable is most often applied, and that application is certainly most important. However, we should never minimize the importance of demonstrating a gospel witness in practical, seemingly non-spiritual ways. Our second-nature impulse should be to feel deeply and serve especially the needs of the unnoticed.

I don't know how, but somehow through my family's and church's influence I picked up that empathetic impulse at a very early age. I remember when I set my teddy bear upright against my pillow as the final act of making my bed each day. I felt sorry for Teddy when I walked out the door to go to school, because he would be there all by himself. I often apologized to him before shutting off the light. As I grew older, my concern for Teddy's loneliness transferred to guys like David, the challenged kid whom classmates mocked, and Steve, one of only two African American kids in my school of hundreds of second-generation white ethnic students with names like Przestrzelski, Reitano, and Franklin Eberhard Gladstone III.

I sensed that being Christian meant passing by the cool kids' lunch table and sitting beside the lone kid with the dingy white T-shirt.

True Christianity … it's always about leaving the ninety-nine with their advantages and privileges and showing special care for *the one*, the unnoticed, the minority—whoever that one may be, wherever that one may be, and whyever that one may be there. Jesus made that clear. It's the heart of this parable; it's the heart of God.

This special care for *the one* is often spiritualized to such a narrow degree that we miss some desperate needs and great opportunities for demonstrating and dispensing God's life-giving love. Let me give you a great example along with a provocative proposal that seems to run counter to conventional wisdom and common practice among God's people.

It's amazing how people of all faiths, political ideologies, ethnicities, and social classes pull together in the aftermath of major natural disasters, like earthquakes, hurricanes, and tornadoes. Local and national media outlets cover the events and their human impact for days and weeks. Professional athletes, Hollywood celebrities, and famous singers launch efforts that raise millions of dollars. Churches and other nonprofit organizations spring into action to send workers and truckloads of donated goods. And of course, government and public relief agencies provide life-saving and rebuilding assistance, usually with mixed reviews but on a massive scale.

The stories of lost loved ones and destroyed homes and businesses tear at our hearts.

> When Ken Fraley emerged from the bathroom where he had sheltered his wife and two small children in the tub under a mattress, he couldn't believe his eyes. He had seen pictures on television after other tornadoes, but nothing prepared him for what it would feel like to open the door and see only the concrete pad and part of the chimney of the once two-story brick farmhouse he and his dad had built together twenty years ago. He hung his head. He wasn't sure how to prepare his family, so he just opened the door a little wider and reached out for his wife's hand.
>
> The kids weren't old enough to understand, but his wife, Jenny, felt flattened by a swirl of thoughts that came all at once in no order of importance: "Is the picture of us at Disney World gone? How can I get the girls to dance class tomorrow? Where's the dog? How are we going to make it with Ken out of work for the past two months? Oh no, my sister's wedding is next week, and she's counting on me for the wedding cake!"

We all know that people caught in these kinds of disasters, as tragic as such situations are, will be the focus of much attention and assistance. Because the governor or president can declare a state of emergency, people like the Fraleys will be eligible for all sorts of relief and resources. New clothes, food, temporary shelter, low-interest loans, and other benefits come from being in the spotlight of national coverage and compassion. But what if I tell you that the Fraleys' loss was an isolated event and not part of a widespread disaster that affected thousands of people? They live way out in the country in western Iowa, and the tornado that destroyed their home touched down for fifteen seconds.

There will be no national media coverage. Sure, they might receive some local attention and gestures of kindness. But they will receive nothing on the scale of help that occurs after a major tornadic storm like the one that flattened Joplin, Missouri, in 2011, and triggered a flood of compassion and care from thousands and thousands of people.

THE SHADOWS OF SINGULARITY

My point is this: all around our nation, when a large enough disaster hits and makes the regional or national news, when hundreds or thousands of people fall victim to winds and waves of destruction, when first responders risk their own lives to rush to their rescue, when cameras and correspondents solicit attention that generates massive relief and rebuilding efforts, the needs get noticed. Yet numerous other families endure similar destruction but are never noticed, because they had the ironic misfortune of not suffering as part of some widespread disaster. Theirs was just one relatively small disaster that did not register the tiniest tremor on anyone's Richter scale.

At the very time bright lights of compassion shine on thousands, people all around our homes and towns and cities suffer just as tragic losses but do so in the shadows of singularity:

- A stray bullet from a gang-related skirmish outside her home pierced Maria Escobar's living room window just above where she was coloring a picture of a unicorn and struck her thirty-eight-year-old mother below her left eye, killing her instantly. She, her little brother, and her mom had recently relocated to St. Louis from San Antonio after an unwanted divorce. Kids who lost a parent during a major disaster will be in the eye of compassionate help. But who's going to notice Maria and her brother? Who will give them a home? A hope? A future?

- Janelle Shipley's husband wandered away ... again. She thought for sure he had been taking his medication but apparently not. She hopped in the car and began driving to all the places she thought he might be. She kept looking at her watch; she was supposed to have been on her way to work fifteen minutes ago. Her boss had warned her, "Another day coming in late and I'm going to have to let you go." But what could she do? Her husband or her job—their only income? She kept driving. If only her husband had gone missing during a major flood while the whole nation was in "rescue mode," her boss might have been more compassionate.

During those times of widespread devastation, when compassion abounds and mobilizes people of all faiths and backgrounds to respond, shouldn't Christians also look for *the one* whose situation will never make the evening news and who will have to face it all alone?

A PROVOCATIVE PROPOSAL

So here's my application of the lost sheep parable. I think it is in harmony with, if not the actual theme of, Jesus' spirit of compassion. When any disaster strikes that gains attention and compels compassionate action and your heart and likely your church want to join the relief efforts in some meaningful way, do this: match your efforts to respond to the spotlighted needs with some effort to find and rescue a person or family who otherwise will not be noticed and will have no help. If you're going to raise relief funds, fill a couple of trailers with emergency supplies and deploy your church van with a team of volunteers to go to the affected city, don't stop there. Match that effort by looking for some unnoticed family in western Iowa— or wherever—that was crushed by some isolated tragedy.

Not long before I began to write this chapter, hurricanes slammed the city of Houston, Texas, and then the entire state of Florida and created historic floods and destruction. The national news media focused on these areas for days—and rightly so. But did you know that during the very same season, devastating floods and landslides hit numerous places in Africa, killing hundreds more people, destroying countless more homes, devastating thousands more families? Probably not. We were focused on Houston and Florida. But what about the unnoticed others? Who will rescue them? Because of our wealthy culture's advantages, the existence and responsiveness of public and private relief agencies, and a strong national government, victims in our nation are like the ninety-nine within the fold of compassionate assistance. What about those who are not?

As a pastor, I have officiated many funerals. Sometimes the bereaved family will notify the public: "In lieu of sending flowers, please make a donation to your favorite charity in memory of our dearly loved husband, father, and grandfather." Their intent is for money to go where it is needed most, toward humanitarian needs rather than flowers.

During major disasters that marshal generous donations and volunteer hours, what if our churches went so far as to say, "In lieu of (or in addition to) sending relief to those major disaster areas, we will honor those wonderful efforts by sending relief to where no help at all is going right now—to places of isolated disaster and people no one is noticing."

I suppose the question still remains: Is Jesus' parable of the lost sheep elastic enough to fit the application I am making? If so, is your compassion elastic enough to wrap around *the one* I am talking about?

20/20 FOCUS

1. Matthew's and Luke's completely different uses of the same parable support the idea that certain portions of Scripture can be properly understood as elastic (i.e., they can be applied in different ways). But what cautions would you offer to make sure we never stretch Scripture too far?

2. There was at least one time when the apostle Peter stretched Scripture to make a point. In Acts 4:11, he changed one three-letter word as he quoted Psalm 118:22. Look up both verses in the NIV to spot that key word. How and why did he stretch that verse to fit the situation he was in?

3. This chapter focuses on the "shadows of singularity." Try to put into your own words what that means.

4. List three or four problems in the media's limelight currently that are receiving lots of attention and triggering lots of social action and human kindness. Then counterbalance that attention by identifying someone suffering (or some kind of problem) no one is noticing.

Lord Jesus, I am grateful for how the regional and national media can rally people to humanitarian causes, especially in times of widespread crisis. But I want my compassion and my church to be controlled and directed by Your Spirit, not the secular media. Give us eyes to see, ears to hear, and the will to act on behalf of those whose situations and suffering have not attracted attention. Amen.

VISION CHECK

God's Word is not rigid. It's alive. That means it can move and stretch. Its truth is fixed, but its application varies. It's elastic enough to cover more than the immediate scriptural context. It's good to imagine other situations to which its truth might apply.

For example, think about the parable of the ten virgins (Matt. 25:1–13). Readers often assume that the immediate application of this parable is to Jesus' return. While that does seem to be the case, think about the main points Jesus was making about these virgins. Imagine how you could apply these principles to circumstances and occasions other than the second coming. Bring your ideas to dougnewton.com or the Fresh Eyes app to compare them with mine.

10

STREETLIGHTS

The Good Samaritan

Luke 10:30–37

What if some parables had a second chapter?

Some people have called me a creative person, especially regarding my writing skills. To whatever degree that's true, I know some of it came from my dad. Not that he was great shakes as a writer. But he had a habit of inventing words—so many words that my two brothers and I put together a *Dictionary of Erfisms* for my parents' fortieth anniversary. *Erfisms?* you wonder. His middle name was Erford. Anyone with a name like that is destined for a life of eccentric elocution as an accidental neologue (one who makes up words). For example:

- *fizgig*: a euphemistic word for a laxative. The mere use of the term usually caused the desired result in my red-faced dad.

- *gingkos*: a versatile term of either endearment or exasperation that follows the exclamation "You …" depending on the prevailing mood of the observer of gingkish behavior.

My dad liked everything neat. He stacked his pocket change in order on the bedroom bureau every night. He thought that even though the English language includes verbs like *bollix*, *muss*, and *jounce*, it is not rich enough to provide words that fit every situation where one is in the act of putting something out of order. So he created new words that offered more precise nuances:

- *shuck*: to make a minute adjustment to the position of any heavy object, as in "Shuck it this way a hair."

- *squudgin*: to twist, shift, or rumple any cloth surface or flexible object. Always follows the command, "Don't …" as in "Don't squudgin the tablecloth."

You may not be someone who makes up quirky words, but most people have a creative streak in some area of their lives. You may be able to look at an empty vase and a handful of wildflowers and "see" how to arrange them into a lovely bouquet. Some people possess an ear for music and have taught themselves how to play piano or guitar. Although most people require detailed recipes when they cook, you might have a knack for experimenting with ingredients and spices to make new dishes.

My wife and I spent many years in the South and marveled at the way some of our friends could transform a simple report about going to the grocery store into an elaborate drama full of action and description that rivaled a bestselling novel. And even though laziness might be the underlying motivation, some people can invent new ways of completing menial tasks more quickly and with less effort. What creative person first thought of carving an inclined plane helically around a cylindrical rod to produce an object that holds wood together? Then some other creative person like my dad came along and invented a name for it: a screw.

One of my major purposes for this book has been to show that most of us could be more creative in our interaction with Scripture if we gave ourselves a little nudge. I want to offer one more example of what I mean and how to do it using the famous parable of the good Samaritan. This classic drama conveys Jesus' answer to the question, "Who is my neighbor?" (Luke 10:29), and is central to the gospel message.

As you know, the parable tells of a victim of a violent robbery who was left to die not only by the thieves themselves but also by two Jewish passersby: a priest and a Levite. Then a despised Samaritan—a character Jesus introduced to shock His Jewish listeners—came along and provided life-saving compassion and comprehensive care.

> A man was going down from Jerusalem to
> Jericho, when he was attacked by robbers. They
> stripped him of his clothes, beat him and went

away, leaving him half dead. A priest happened to be going down the same road, and when he saw the man, he passed by on the other side. So too, a Levite, when he came to the place and saw him, passed by on the other side. But a Samaritan, as he traveled, came where the man was; and when he saw him, he took pity on him. He went to him and bandaged his wounds, pouring on oil and wine. Then he put the man on his own donkey, brought him to an inn and took care of him. The next day he took out two denarii and gave them to the innkeeper. "Look after him," he said, "and when I return, I will reimburse you for any extra expense you may have." (vv. 30–35)

Clearly, Jesus painted a portrait of self-sacrificing, risk-taking love as the only true fulfillment of the law of love. For generations God's people have examined under a magnifying glass every detail of this incredible picture of mercy and grace.

It's worth trying to understand why the priest and Levite did nothing to help. And we often try. The Samaritan's multi-faceted act of compassion and rescue should be analyzed and imitated by every Christian in every generation in every cultural context. And we have those components—emergency response, thorough care, and ongoing support—clearly spelled out. The way Jesus used a Samaritan as an unlikely hero was one of His many attacks on ethnic prejudice. It highlights a primary goal of the gospel toward which Christians are called to work: to tear down *all* dividing walls of hostility, not just ones between God and people and between Jews and Gentiles (Eph. 2:14–16). Retrofitting the story for a new generation and culture is appropriate creative interaction with the text, and it is done often and done well.

EXPERIMENTAL VARIATIONS

However, there's another way to interact creatively with biblical texts that I call "experimental variations." Scientists do this in their research. As they test hypotheses, they change one component of the experiment, called the variable, and observe what happens. What happens if we heat the solution five degrees more? What happens if we heat the solution before we mix in the chlorine rather than after? What happens if we freeze the solution and store it for twenty-four hours before we heat it? They learn new things by making slight adjustments.

Similarly, experimental variations to a particular biblical passage can trigger creative interactions with the text and with God's Spirit that produce fresh insights. Ask yourself, *What would happen if I changed just one story component?* Let's do that with this parable by imagining what happened the days *after* the Samaritan rescued the victim and resumed his journey. You'll see how that raises a new set of questions about how love should act.

THE NEXT THREE DAYS

Imagine the following scenario: the Samaritan mounted his donkey and headed once again toward Jericho. He passed the place where he had rescued the wounded traveler, grateful to God for his opportunity to save a person's life.

Not more than a mile farther down the road, he couldn't believe his eyes when he saw the form of another wounded traveler lying beside the road. When he saw him, he took pity on him and showed the same care to this traveler as he had to the one the day before.

The innkeeper was somewhat surprised to see the Samaritan bringing another wounded victim to his inn for care. But again the businessman was promised a return visit and reimbursement for any expenses beyond another two denarii (silver coins).

The Samaritan stayed the night and left the next morning, but not before taking a minute to count his money and calculate whether he had enough left for the time he planned to spend in Jericho.

By now he was two days overdue for his business in Jericho, and he hoped his friends would not be worrying about him. So he picked up his pace to make up for lost time.

About three hours down the road, but less than halfway, his heart sank when he saw in the distance the form of another man lying in the road. Worry shot through his mind: *I can't believe this. Could this be yet another victim?*

Sure enough. It was! *What shall I do? My time and money are running out.* He wished he hadn't noticed the victim. But there he lay in the middle of the road. There was no getting around the reality. He saw the wounds, heard the man's faint cry, and compassion welled up inside him, so he stopped, dressed the wounds, lifted the man onto his donkey, and returned to the inn.

The innkeeper, now quite confused and perhaps a little suspicious, reluctantly gave another room to yet another victim— reluctantly because the Samaritan now had to ask for special considerations, since he could not advance the innkeeper any money. He could only promise to pay the bill on his return. The innkeeper was not at all pleased.

The next morning, under considerable pressure from how his tardiness jeopardized his business and reputation, the Samaritan rode as fast as possible toward Jericho again. He felt deeply troubled. *What if I see another wounded traveler?* The worry did not let up. Step after step, he feared what was around the next curve. *I cannot be delayed again!*

Then sure enough, from a man lying off in the bushes, he heard a faint moan for help. "No way! I can't do this anymore!" the Samaritan shouted in agony, as he looked with longing to the other side of the road.

There you have it—an experimental variation on this famous parable that makes one hypothetical adjustment to the story: What if the same thing happened to the Samaritan numerous times, not just once? This question is worth asking for several reasons.

A VALID VARIATION

Basic research on the actual text reveals that this road was known to be very dangerous. It is reasonable to wonder how a person might respond to more than one occurrence of a desperate rescue situation. So it's historically valid.

It's also emotionally valid. My experimental Samaritan represents what people soon discover when they commit themselves to lives of compassion for the needy: the desperate problems never let up and soon threaten to drain them dry of time and resources. Even the most compassionate people are prone to pass by like the priest and Levite out of sheer exhaustion.

Finally, it is conceptually valid. The parable Jesus told answered not only the question "Who is my neighbor?" but also "How does true love behave?" Jesus painted the picture of thorough and tender caregiving. My experimental version that imagines the realistic possibility of serial robberies puts fresh eyes on this compassion question. How does love behave in cases of chronic violence and victimization?

GREATER MEASURES

Put yourself in the experimental Samaritan's situation. By the time he had faced the same problem three times, and now a fourth, what might he begin to think? *I need a solution other than just loading these people on my donkey and trying to rescue them all by myself.* This is where the fresh eyes technique of "experimental variations" takes us: to deal with the fact that real life often presents us with rescue challenges that one person can't handle alone. In other words, love faces the prospect of ineffectiveness and refuses to stop until it develops strategies to solve bigger problems.

Think about that for a minute. If you faced this experimental but true-to-life situation, what solutions might love propose? Two strategic solutions come to my mind.

Rescue Teams

The experimental Samaritan needs help. He needs a team of on-call people who share his sense of compassion and his conviction that prioritizes desperate people's needs over his own. He would need to create an organization to take responsibility for developing and deploying that kind of person into the … Oh, wait a minute. I think one already exists. It's called the church.

Now do you see how this fresh eyes technique logically leads to another creative way of looking at the parable? Go back to the parable and ask these questions: What insights might I gain if I think of the priest, Levite, and Samaritan as different types of churches and the victim as a type of human need? What is my church avoiding or too busy to notice? Do our benevolence ministries go far enough to fully care for and restore damaged people? Yes, we serve a meal at Thanksgiving to needy people, but does that really do much to alleviate their struggle to make ends meet? In other words, take all the ideas that are commonly taught about the ways individuals should show love to broken people—emergency response, thorough care, and ongoing support—and apply them to your church.

So, for example, among the greatest problems that trap people in economic poverty is consumer debt. People trapped in consumer debt are like people who can never keep their heads above water, because their bills keep pushing them back under. For years, my wife and I have encouraged God's people to model gospel love by periodically helping to pay other people's credit card debts to give them a chance to keep their heads above water. We believe in this.

In his book *The Working Poor: Invisible in America*, Pulitzer Prize–winning author David Shipler documented how the smallest problems, like the need for eyeglasses or dental work, can derail working people's attempts to rise above poverty.[1] When we come alongside a family and offer to make monthly payments on one of their debts until it is paid off, that usually frees them up so they can get their car repaired and get to work, pay for more reliable childcare, or accelerate their debt reduction in other areas. Although it's not a cure for poverty, this not only helps provide a better chance for them to keep their heads above water and gradually make it to dry ground, but it also is one of the best ways to demonstrate the nature of the cross of Christ: substitutionary debt payment. That is, Jesus paid our debt on our behalf.

Streetlights

If people keep getting robbed and beaten on the road, then put up streetlights! Even though this solution falls into the category of "Duh," the church often overlooks streetlight strategies (i.e., prevention programs). We should show love through prevention as much as through rescue. In fact, even if you successfully develop and deploy hundreds of teams of rescuers but do nothing to address the cause, you have not done what compassion ultimately calls for—protecting people from harm.

Prevention efforts are usually not as sexy, as they say. But the city councilperson who crafts and champions legislation for funding city streetlights to protect hundreds of people in high-crime areas is engaging in an act of love perhaps greater than the Good Samaritan's. Keeping young girls from being seized for sex trafficking is to be desired over having to rescue them after being broken. Love that prevents wounds should usually be preferred over love that tends them. Of course, God sometimes chooses not to prevent pain or hardships in order to reveal His glory through people by developing their godly character or displaying divine power. But generally speaking, divine love agrees with Ben Franklin's classic words of wisdom written when he campaigned for fire safety: "An Ounce of Prevention is worth a Pound of Cure."[2]

In the previous chapter, I mentioned that around the same time the flooding in Houston in 2017 captured our national attention, hundreds more people died from flooding and landslides in Africa. The enormous effects of the Texas hurricane could not have been prevented. But many of the African floods could have been, because they were due not to a massive hurricane but to poor drainage systems. It was commendable that our public, private, and nonprofit organizations poured relief resources into Texas, but churches especially should be looking across the oceans and tackling the prevention needs in chronically under-resourced areas where deadly disasters could be minimized.

Just as the church answers the call to develop and deploy rescuers, we need to equally emphasize the ministries of prevention. And we need to applaud the people in our congregations who engage in prevention missions as much as those involved in rescue work. People who devote themselves to making other people safer, people who commit themselves to education and job training, people who prayer-walk their communities and initiate reconciliation projects are all doing kingdom work that's like installing streetlights in a dark and dangerous world.

BACK TO THE STARTING POINT

Do you see how this fresh eyes technique opens the window to a host of thoughts you might never have had without creatively thinking beyond the limits of the actual text? Of course, when engaging in creative interaction with Scripture, you must be careful to remember—or research—what's scriptural and what's not. Never entertain ideas that contradict other biblical texts and truths. However, in this case, there is value in opening the aperture wider to let this parable shed more light on how love should behave.

But finally, that raises a question. If broadening this parable beyond the text's original scope in order to see that prevention and not just rescue is important, why did Jesus limit the parable to one Samaritan rescuing one victim? My guess is He left the story where He did to confront us with an unconditional personal challenge. Ultimately the systemic changes needed to rescue people and prevent evil on a larger scale depend on the existence and responsiveness of individuals who love like the good Samaritan in one-on-one missions of mercy and grace.

My dad had a name for a person like that—a "good egg."

20/20 FOCUS

1. Compassionate disciples sometimes want to walk "on the other side" of the street to get a break from people's problems. Once we start caring about hurting people, it seems like there's no end. In those times we can feel frustrated, angry, disillusioned, discouraged, or extremely fatigued. Do any of these feelings describe where you are at this point? Which one(s)?

2. Jesus clearly wanted us to notice the thorough steps of compassion the Samaritan took. Think of some type of prevention ministry (e.g., preventing divorce, preventing consumer debt, or preventing teen pregnancy) and list some steps that are necessary if those ministries are to be thorough and effective.

3. Name a couple of problems where you (or your church) are in rescue mode but you wish you were doing more about prevention.

Lord Jesus, I'll admit I can be like the priest and Levite and want to avoid people who need help.

I've gotten to the point where I am tired and discouraged. The needs keep coming, but I've run out. I'd love to feel I'm doing more than providing bandages. Could You point me in the direction of some new effort that might promote prevention? I'd love to pour some of my limited energy and resources into that. But still, give me the grace to bandage wounds. Amen.

VISION CHECK

In scientific experiments you introduce one new variable to discover something you didn't known before. You can guardedly do the same with Scripture. In this chapter, we imagined what the Good Samaritan might need to do had he come across multiple victims over the span of several days. If you try this, remember that the variable is not in the text, so you shouldn't turn your thoughts into a "new doctrine." But you might gain some new insights worth pondering in light of other portions of Scripture.

Try this: read John's version of the feeding of the five thousand, which includes the interesting detail about the five loaves and two fish coming from a boy (John 6:1–15). Try imagining what might have happened if the boy had only three loaves and one fish to bring. Then try another variation of the amount. What thoughts come to mind? Compare your thoughts with mine on dougnewton.com or the Fresh Eyes app.

NOTES

INTRODUCTION

1. C. H. Dodd, *The Parables of the Kingdom*, rev. ed. (New York: Charles Scribner's Sons, 1961), 5.

2. Craig L. Blomberg, *Interpreting the Parables*, 2nd ed. (Downers Grove, IL: InterVarsity Press, 2012), 35.

CHAPTER 1

1. George Frideric Handel, "Hallelujah Chorus," Lyrics.com, accessed February 5, 2018, www.lyrics.com/lyric/324457.

CHAPTER 6

1. Edward Mote, "My Hope Is Built," Cyberhymnal.org, accessed February 5, 2018, http://cyberhymnal.org/htm/m/y/myhopeis.html.

CHAPTER 8

1. George MacDonald, *Diary of an Old Soul: 366 Writings for Devotional Reflection* (Mansfield Centre, CT: Martino, 2015), August 11.

2. Dylan Thomas, "Do Not Go Gentle into That Good Night," in *The Poems of Dylan Thomas*, ed. Daniel Jones (New York: New Directions, 2003), 239.

CHAPTER 10

1. David K. Shipler, *The Working Poor: Invisible in America* (New York: Vintage, 2005), 52–53.

2. Benjamin Franklin, "On Prevention of Towns from Fire," *Pennsylvania Gazette*, February 4, 1735, https://founders.archives.gov/documents /Franklin/01-02-02-0002.

1

WHAT MAKES THE OLD CROSS SO RUGGED?

Take Up Your Cross

Luke 9:23

If we're supposed to follow Jesus, we'd better make sure we know what His cross is like.

Do we really think the best way to prove God's love is to splash blood all over the crucifixion story? We essentially do all year long but especially during the Easter season. When preachers want to hammer home the enormity of Jesus' sacrifice, they often resort to giving detailed descriptions of His suffering. They try to do verbally what Mel Gibson did visually in his 2004 blockbuster *The Passion of the Christ*. Who could watch without wincing? Gibson took us inside Jesus' torn flesh deeper than we wanted to go. Sermons can't match cinema.

But we try. Preachers describe the whips that tore Jesus' flesh. They point to where the nails were likely driven in—through the wrists, not the palms—and why: Jesus' body weight would have ripped His hands loose between His middle and ring fingers. Attempting to add visual emphasis to the verbal explanation, they demonstrate with their bodies how being hung in that fashion would have constricted His airways. In order to take a breath, Jesus would have had to push down on the nails driven through His feet. Excruciating.

Some drag out the description to simulate the length of Jesus' suffering, until they finally talk about the spear and the watery blood gushing as the spear's tip penetrated the pericardial sac, adding notes of medical science to make it sound more believable, more factual. All this is designed to attract the listener to God's love through the most repulsive image of death imaginable.

You've likely heard similar descriptions as well. Ironically, such painful portrayals have helped create a severe misunderstanding of the nature of the cross we are supposed to "take up" in order to follow Jesus. To a degree, understanding what a crucifixion really involved—and what Jesus likely endured—may help some listeners both grasp God's love and understand something unfamiliar to our culture. As such, preachers who teach this way do so with commendable motivations. However, a heavy-handed, unbalanced focus on Christ's suffering can lead to some significant, though unintended, misunderstandings.

NOT JUST ANY KIND OF SUFFERING

When preachers belabor the many horrific elements of Jesus' death, it is understandable that people primarily equate the cross with suffering. Consequently, we tend to perceive any unwanted or unfair suffering as our "cross to bear." Whether we encounter a thoughtless person at work or a traumatic experience, we may pray about such things, but most of us still think there's simply nothing to be done about them. It's injustice that God wants us to learn from. Didn't Jesus warn us there'd be trials?

Yet suffering in and of itself, even for godly reasons or with a godly attitude, does not necessarily constitute the cross of Christ. Perhaps you are finding it hard to imagine a Christian even saying this. How can this be?

Simple. Something is missing. The true cross has a specific purpose: accepting the burden of suffering in order to provide a remedy for the suffering of others. Jesus paid the penalty for our sin by taking our place. When Jesus was sentenced to death, He had committed no wrong. He deserved no punishment. We, on the other hand, owed God an unpayable debt because of our many, many sins committed out of negligence, ignorance, disobedience, and rebellion. The death sentence hung justly over our heads. When Jesus hung on the cross, He suffered the consequences of our failures, pure and simple, so we could be forgiven. Our sin wasn't His fault, His problem, or due to His neglect. Yet He paid the price. He exchanged places with us. He provided the remedy at great personal cost. As Paul put it, "God made him who had no sin to be sin for us, so that in him we might become the righteousness of God" (2 Cor. 5:21).

This is the true character of the cross. It can be stated simply: something isn't a cross until you are paying a personal price to provide a remedy for someone else's suffering whether due to sin, foolishness, or misfortune. So when a person crosses the street to help a neighbor through a financial crisis after getting fired from his job or when missionaries cross the ocean, taking their kids away from grandparents and familiar surroundings, to serve an unreached people group, they are following the way of the cross.

Only when we give up something rightfully ours or put ourselves in harm's way or jeopardize our security for another is it like Jesus' cross—and even then, it only faintly reflects what He endured.

The unsettling thought is that Jesus seems to expect us to do this—*daily!* Even if we could, do we honestly have that many opportunities? I believe we do. There are sometimes dramatic ones, but more often, there are simple daily interactions. But they're always divine moments.

THE CROSS MAY SOMETIMES BE DRAMATIC

As a college freshman, I became our college newspaper's assistant editor. I wanted to be the editor in my sophomore year, but underclassmen weren't allowed to hold that position. I appealed for an exception and was granted approval, provided I study under the editor that year—a college senior.

In a bewildering turn of events, he made a bizarre sexual request of me. I refused, and he threatened suicide if I did not grant his request. Frightened but resolute, I refused again.

Later that week, with the editor present, I informed the faculty adviser of my decision to resign, forfeiting my opportunity to be editor. I remember that night vividly. The adviser was frustrated because he had gone to bat for me to get the rules changed. "Why?" he wondered.

But I wouldn't say why. I knew it was a sacrifice. The editor was agnostic, and I knew his reputation would be ruined if I shared. So I remained silent. But the editor jumped in and bitterly "explained" that my change of heart was due to immaturity and other severe character flaws.

The adviser turned to me, bewildered. "How can you just sit there?" he asked. "If someone was saying about me what he's saying about you, I'd hit him in the mouth."

Wanting to be Christlike in that moment, not sure I was doing the right thing—and even though speaking up is often critically important—I believed in this case my silence and sacrifice, even if ultimately unnecessary, would honor Jesus and He could use it somehow. So I entrusted myself to the One who judges justly and renounced my position on the college newspaper staff.

I completed my college career with a cloud over my head, my reputation damaged. But ten years later that editor wrote me a letter apologizing and sharing his newfound faith, attributing it largely to my testimony of silence under false accusation. And although I thought that episode derailed my track toward journalism, twenty years later, with no further journalistic experience, my denomination unexpectedly asked me to be the editor of its national magazine. It was like a resurrection took place, which mirrored what taking up a true cross should ultimately produce, though often no such direct restoration for our sacrifices seems forthcoming.

THE CROSS OCCURS DAILY

I share that dramatic story to offer hope. We don't always know what to do or whether our decisions for Jesus' way will even matter in the end. But we face choices every day to give up something we may never regain (time, money, credit) to provide something others may never deserve (grace, forgiveness, a second chance). That's the cross.

How do you know when you've arrived at one of these daily "take up your cross" moments? Your insides will resonate and moan with a single question: *Why should I have to be the one?* We hear this voice in small ways every day.

No one ever takes a class to learn this line. Kids aren't taught it in kindergarten like the Pledge of Allegiance. Yet there's probably never been a human being who hasn't said those words exactly, word for word, in his or her native language: *Why should I have to be the one?*

Just as a streak of lightning illuminates your home for a split second, your internal sense of justice instantly highlights the unfairness: *I wasn't the one who made the mistake. I'm not the one to blame.* We reasonably fear enabling mistreatment and worse.

I'm always having to make up for what she doesn't do.

I'm the one always bending over backward.

He never says he's sorry. If we ever make up, it's because I initiate it.

She almost always misses her deadline; then I'm left with too little time and look bad.

But there is no way around it. The true cross of Jesus calls you to lose what you may never regain to give what others may never deserve. And perhaps—but only perhaps—others will see the love of God demonstrated through your grace.

These kinds of situations happen every day, particularly ones involving your use of time and resources. The cross is accepting unfairness. It's receiving poor treatment. It's not fighting back.

THE CROSS WILL ALWAYS BE DIVINE

Taking up the true cross can also mean taking on others' pain when they're victims of improper treatment or have made innocent mistakes.

Years ago, my wife took some city kids on a field trip to the country to expose them to the wonders of nature. She led them high and low through the woods, spying plants, tiny flowers, birds, and bugs. They carved names on tree fungus and made hiking sticks. It was a wonderful couple of hours, until she got back to the landowners' home. When she told them where the kids had gone, they gasped. "Oh no, you took them right through undergrowth full of poison ivy!"

My wife felt heartsick. To think that her desire to inspire them to love nature might actually leave them stricken with terrible allergic reactions and a fear of nature! But in that moment, a hope shot through her—an impression of something, maybe the only thing she could do. Pray. And not just any prayer, but a costly one. "Lord," she prayed, "please protect the kids. If any of them got poison ivy, put it all on me so none of them suffers with it."

Wouldn't you know, the next day poison ivy welted her arms and legs—the worst case she ever had—but none of the kids ever broke out. I don't pretend to understand how and why the Lord chooses to work as He does. But I did wonder, *If He could do that, couldn't He have rid poison ivy from them all without my wife breaking out?* Such questions are hard to answer definitively. However, the apostle Paul pointed us in the right direction when he shared that he thirsted to know Jesus to such a degree that everything else in his life amounted to nothing more than garbage in comparison. As he saw it, "knowing Christ" involves experiencing resurrection power. But it also includes the other side of the coin: "I consider everything a loss because of the surpassing worth of knowing Christ Jesus my Lord, for whose sake I have lost all things…. I want to know Christ—yes, to know and the power of his resurrection and *participation in his sufferings*, becoming like him in his death" (Phil. 3:8, 10).

I know no one more Christlike than my wife. I believe Jesus made her that way. He's making all of us that way. When we suffer for others' sake—whether innocent victims or guilty villains—we enter into His suffering and become like Him. Why would Jesus want to short-circuit that?

It doesn't take preachers splashing blood to make the cross a wonder to behold. It just takes people like my wife showing what the cross is like.

20/20 FOCUS

1. When we suffer in the place of another person, we are truly taking up the cross of Christ. But that doesn't mean other times of suffering are pointless. What other reasons may God have for allowing us to suffer?

2. Why do you think we tend to miss the central nature of the cross—taking on someone else's suffering—when it comes to carrying our cross?

3. This chapter mentions a few examples of daily opportunities to take on the consequences of other people's neglect or mistakes. Can you think of a few examples from your own life or the life of someone you know?

Lord, now that I have a sharper focus on the nature of the cross I am supposed to carry, I realize why You mentioned self-denial first. I never will be able to take up a cross like Yours unless You fulfill the purpose of Your cross in me: set me free from selfishness and fill my heart with Your self-sacrificing love. Amen.

VISION CHECK

A secondary element in a Scripture passage or biblical event that has come to dominate our attention can sometimes overshadow a passage's main point as in this case, in which the popular emphasis on the violence done to Jesus has come to overshadow the purpose of His suffering. Always ask yourself, *What is the primary element in this text or event?*

Read the creation account in Genesis 1, noting its chronological structure. For years the question of a six-day creation process has dominated people's attention. Debates rage and so do people over this issue. Is this a secondary or primary issue in the biblical account? What else might deserve to be raised to a primary position of attention and application? If you make that the issue of greatest importance, do you see the creation account in a new way? See my discoveries by going to dougnewton.com or the Fresh Eyes app.

FRESH
EYES

VISIT
WWW.DOUGNEWTON.COM

- Learn more and connect with the author
- Be the first to learn about new projects
- Find out if Doug is speaking near you
- Get brand new, fresh content